CENTENNIAL BOOKS

THE TRUE STORY OF SANTA CLAUS

By Janet Giovanelli

CONTENTS

Chapter 2
CLAUS-IAN CUSTOMS

50 WHY SANTA DODGES THE FRONT DOOR
The history of St. Nick sliding down the chimney to deliver gifts goes back centuries.

52 DEAR SANTA
How an illustrator and a burgeoning post office gave children a direct line to St. Nick.

98

Gingerbread men date back to 16th century England.

166

124

Chapter 1
ORIGINS OF THE SANTA LEGEND

10 ALL ABOUT SANTA
St. Nick may seem like a timeless figure, but his legend has evolved over the millennia.

22 MEET MRS. CLAUS
Behind every good man is a great woman, and Santa Claus is no exception.

30 SANTA'S HELPERS
The elves are an integral part of the Christmas story.

38 HOW SANTA GOT HIS REINDEER
An in-depth look at the Arctic sleigh-pullers.

44 MYSTERY SOLVED
Ever wonder how Kris Kringle gets to everyone's house in one night? Read this story!

46 HO, HO, HO, HE'S ON THE GO, GO, GO!
Sure, his sleigh is supreme, but it's not the only way this gift-giver gets from here to there.

Some overseas traditions, like the "poop log," are a little out there! →

88

58 POMP & CIRCUMSTANCE FOR ST. NICK
Since 1924, the Macy's Thanksgiving Day Parade has marked the start of the season.

60 STUFFED STOCKINGS
This custom dates back nearly 2,000 years!

64 MERRY MEET & GREETS
There's a generous store owner to thank for making children's dreams come true.

68 O CHRISTMAS TREE
Evergreens have long been a part of the holiday season.

76 CHRISTMAS GREETINGS
Over 2 billion cards are sent in the U.S. each year.

80 SANTA THROUGH THE YEARS
A glimpse at Hallmark cards over the past century.

84 COOKIES FOR KRINGLE
Christmas isn't just about getting gifts; it's also about giving them, in the form of sweet treats!

88 GOING GLOBAL
A look at Santa figures from all around the world.

Chapter 3
SANTA IN POP CULTURE

100 THE BEST (AND WORST) CELLULOID SANTAS
Portrayals of St. Nick range from magical to malevolent.

112 PICTURE PERFECT
The works of illustrators and painters have greatly shaped Santa's image.

116 THE BEST OF SANTA ON THE SMALL SCREEN
A roundup of the best TV specials of the season.

124 EVERYONE WANTS TO BE HIM
If imitation is the sincerest form of flattery, Santa must be the most adulated of all!

126 LEGENDARY PITCHMAN
From soda to smartphones, Santa Claus has been used to sell a plethora of products.

134 SING A SONG OF SANTA
Christmas music helps get us ready for the Big Guy's arrival.

140 THE CHRONICLES OF KRIS KRINGLE
For centuries, creative tellings of Father Christmas have leapt off the page and into our hearts.

Chapter 4
CLAUS & COMPANY

146 TOYS FOR GIRLS & BOYS
Take a peek inside Santa's sack to discover the most requested presents through the decades.

160 AT HOME WITH SANTA
We invite St. Nick into our living rooms every year. Now it's our turn to take peek inside his abode.

166 CHRISTMAS A TO Z
All about 26 of our favorite Yuletide traditions.

176 SANTA SCHOOL
What does it take to be one of St. Nick's mall helpers? More than you think!

182 SANTAS BY THE SLEIGHFUL
Collectors share their prized possessions with us.

Barbie has been a staple under the tree since 1959. ↘

Ed Asner's Santa had to break it to Buddy, in the movie *Elf*, that his dad was on the Naughty List. ↙

146

100

22

THE MAGIC OF SANTA CLAUS

"Christmas isn't just a day, it's a frame of mind," as Kris Kringle reminds us in the iconic 1947 film *Miracle on 34th Street*. And no one helps us capture that mood more than the man himself. So much more than just a storied gift-giver, he's a symbol of hope and happiness, of generosity and benevolence. Santa Claus is simply one of the most beloved legends our country has ever embraced.

Sure, you cherish him, but how much do you *really* know about the jolly old elf?

This festive, celebratory book will explore the history of Father Christmas. Who is he, really? Where did he come from? (His origins may surprise you!) Why does he fulfill the wishes of nice girls and boys? And what can we learn from him?

We all know that behind every good man is a woman. And Santa is no exception. Read on to learn about Mrs. Claus and the rest of Santa's team of helpers, the elves and his reindeer; how they became part of the legend; and what their roles are today.

There are so many traditions—and mysteries—associated with Santa Claus. Did you ever wonder why he dodges the front door in favor of a chimney? What about those who don't have a chimney? Why does he fill our stockings with gifts, when he already leaves presents under the tree? Speaking of trees, why do we put one in our homes? And perhaps the most perplexing question of all: How does he get to every child in the world in one night? In the pages that follow, you will find the answers to all these questions and so much more.

Much of what we know of the roly-poly guy in red has come from depictions in pop culture. We explore them all: We rank the best movie Santas of all time (and call out those who weren't worthy of wearing the suit); recall the holiday TV specials that have left an indelible mark on the culture of Christmas; examine the catchy jingles that undeniably elevate holiday spirit, year after year; and ponder St. Nick's place in literature, art and advertising.

This entertaining look at the man, the myth, the legend that is Santa Claus is sure to deliver the magic of Christmas straight to your heart.

CHAPTER 1

ORIGINS OF THE SANTA LEGEND

DISCOVER THE FASCINATING BACKSTORIES OF ST. NICK AND ALL OF HIS EXTRAORDINARY HELPERS.

ALL ABOUT SANTA

SANTA CLAUS MAY SEEM LIKE A TIMELESS FIGURE, BUT HIS LEGEND HAS EVOLVED OVER THE MILLENNIA FROM THE BELOVED ST. NICHOLAS TO THE CHERISHED·AND JOLLY BOWL-FULL-OF-JELLY-BELLY GUY WE LOVE TODAY.

Before he began making annual appearances at Macy's, before *Elf* and *Miracle on 34th Street,* before anyone saw Mommy kissing him, before he was an ornament or a chocolate or a cookie cutter, before he was even called Santa...there was a guy called St. Nicholas. St. Nick lived in the fourth century, in what today is part of Turkey, not at the North Pole, so he didn't have reindeer, a sleigh or a fur-trimmed suit. An archbishop, he did wear red robes and had a long white beard.

And he shared one other important Santa trait: His generosity was exemplary. Most famously, when he heard about a poor widower who couldn't afford dowries for his three daughters, St. Nick surreptitiously dropped three bags of gold through an open window in their house in the middle of the night. As one of the most popular saints, his feast day, December 6, was celebrated throughout the Christian world.

The Evolution of St. Nicholas

But today's Santa isn't just a modern version of St. Nicholas; he's a mash-up of various Nicholas legends, pagan midwinter traditions, Nordic and German gods and, finally, the concerted efforts of American civic leaders, artists and ad executives who made him the worldwide phenomenon he is today.

Sinterklaas, the Dutch Santa

It was in Holland in the Middle Ages that Nicholas (known as Sinterklaas in Dutch) began the transition from Saint to Santa. Modern-day Sinterklaas still looks like an archbishop—he wears a long, red cape and a bishop's alb and holds a gold crosier. Every year, he makes a ceremonial entry by boat into the Netherlands in mid-November. (He is said to live in Spain the rest of the year.) Sinterklaas rides a white horse across the sky at

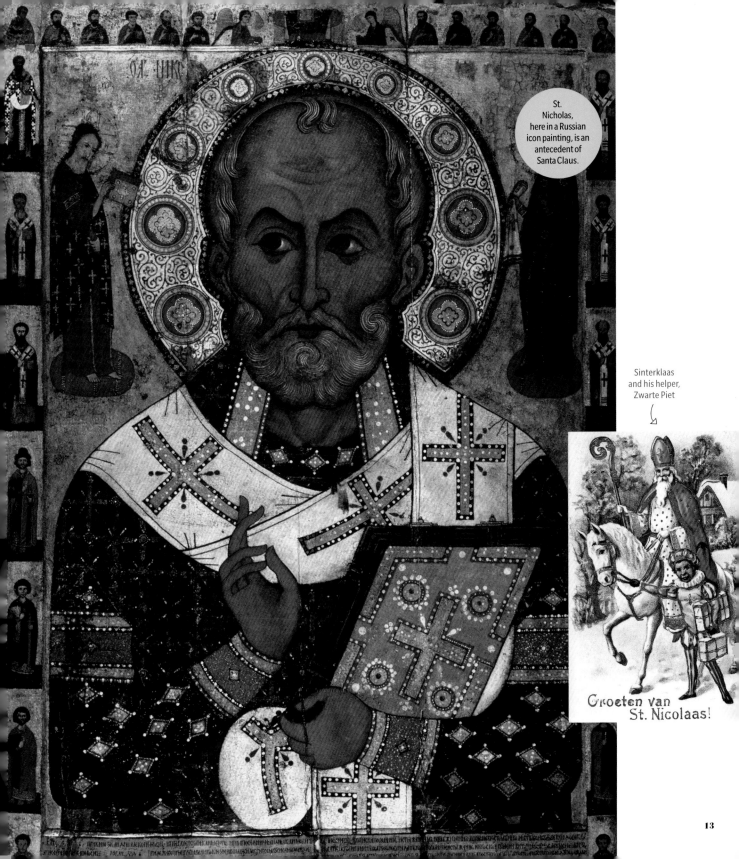

St. Nicholas, here in a Russian icon painting, is an antecedent of Santa Claus.

Sinterklaas and his helper, Zwarte Piet

Groeten van St. Nicolaas!

13

night (a plot twist borrowed from the Germanic god Wodan, aka the Norse god Odin). His assistant, Black Peter (Zwarte Piet), keeps track of children's behavior year-round, so that the "good" ones can be rewarded with toys, cookies and candy in their wooden shoes. (The "bad" kids get the switch from Black Peter. Yikes!) For adults, the Sinterklaas festivities are raucous street parties marked by drunkenness and debauchery.

It was the Protestant reformer Martin Luther who shifted the focus from St. Nicholas Day on December 6 to Christmas. (Wanting to end Catholicism's veneration of the saints, he decided to make Christmas, which focused on Jesus, the major gift-giving holiday.)

A Star Is Born: Santa in America

Two centuries before America's collective obsession with fame led to the Kardashians and the *Real Housewives* casts becoming household names, it

In 1809, in *A Knickerbocker's History of New York*, Washington Irving described St. Nicholas as a "jolly old Dutchman."

Fourteen years after it was first published, "A Visit from St. Nicholas" was attributed to Clement C. Moore.

In 1810, New Yorker John Pintard suggested that the city celebrate St. Nicholas Day.

'Twas the night before Christmas, when all through
    the house
Not a creature was stirring, not even a mouse;
The stockings were hung by the chimney with care,
In hopes that St. Nicholas soon would be there;
The children were nestled all snug in their beds,
While visions of sugar-plums danced in their heads;
And Mamma in her 'kerchief, and I in my cap,
Had just settled our brains for a long winter's nap;
When out on the lawn there arose such a clatter,
I sprang from the bed to see what what was the matter.
Away to the window I flew like a flash,
Tore open the shutters and threw up the sash.
The moon, on the breast of the new-fallen snow,
Gave the lustre of mid-day to objects below,
When, what to my wondering eyes should appear,
But a miniature sleigh, and eight tiny rein-deer,
With a little old driver, so lively and quick,
I knew in a moment it must be St. Nick.
More rapid than eagles his coursers they came,
And he whistled, and shouted, and called them by name;
"Now, _Dasher_! now, _Dancer_! now, _Prancer_ and _Vixen_!
On, _Comet_! on, _Cupid_! on, _Donder_ and _Blitzen_!
To the top of the porch! to the top of the wall!
Now dash away! dash away! dash away all!"

"Santa Behind the Window" was created for *The Saturday Evening Post* by J.C. Leyendecker in 1919.

"Santa at the Globe" was painted in 1926 by Leyendecker's successor, Norman Rockwell.

"He had a broad face, and a little round belly that shook when he laugh'd, like a bowl full of jelly..."

"A VISIT FROM ST. NICHOLAS"

made a celebrity out of a fourth-century saint. The Dutch had migrated to the New World, particularly New York, starting in the 17th century; in the early 1800s, there was a surge of interest in promoting Dutch customs, which led to a revival of St. Nicholas Day/Sinterklaas festivities. Around 1804, John Pintard, a founder of the New-York Historical Society, even began floating the idea of making St. Nicholas the patron saint of New York City. Though that never happened, St. Nick became a different kind of luminary thanks to another founding member of the New-York Historical Society (and Pintard's cousin), Washington Irving.

Irving depicted a more secular, modern version of St. Nicholas in his 1809 book, *A Knickerbocker's History of New York* (written under the pseudonym Diedrich Knickerbocker). He updated Santa's look, replacing the austere bishop in red robes with a jolly-looking Dutch-sailor type whose *green* winter coat was tight across his ample beer belly and who rode a horse-drawn wagon above the treetops. (Irving's book also contains five Christmas stories depicting other scenes that would become Christmas tradition—jovial English-influenced festivities, with large roasts, caroling, decorations and a blazing fire in the fireplace.)

The Man Who Made Santa Claus a Superstar

But the most important thing to happen to the Santa legend since St. Nick tossed that bag full of gold into the widower's house occurred in 1823. That was the year "A Visit from St. Nicholas," better known today as "'Twas the Night Before Christmas," was first published, anonymously, in a Troy, New York, newspaper. (Though Clement C. Moore later claimed authorship, others believe Henry Livingston Jr. was the poem's writer.)

"A Visit from St. Nicholas" drew on Irving's St. Nick as well as "Old Santeclaus with Much Delight," an illustrated children's poem that had been published two years earlier. "Old Santeclaus" had established a few other enduring Santa traditions: his connection with winter, the sleigh

Cartoonist Thomas Nast drew Santa Claus for *Harper's Weekly* 33 times between 1863 and 1886.

A Thomas Nast illustration, circa 1889, shows Santa Claus onstage, pulling back a curtain to reveal fairy-tale characters.

pulled by reindeer and his arrival on Christmas Eve rather than on St. Nicholas Day.

Moore added other details to the Santa legend—St. Nick lands his sleigh on the roof, then slides down the chimney with a sack of toys on his back. He named all of Santa's reindeer (except Rudolph) and linked St. Nick/Santa with Christmas while making clear his jolly, friendly nature:

"His eyes—how they twinkled! His dimples how merry! His cheeks were like roses, his nose like a cherry! His droll little mouth was drawn up like a bow, and the beard of his chin was as white as the snow; the stump of a pipe he held tight in his teeth, and the smoke, it encircled his head like a wreath;

He had a broad face and a little round belly, That shook when he laughed like a bowl full of jelly. He was chubby and plump, a right jolly old elf..."

The poem, which has been touted as "arguably the best-known verses ever written by an American," was reprinted in newspapers for many years, and then in numerous book versions as well as songs and a TV special. Even today, it remains the most influential Santa propaganda.

Santa Gets a Makeover

While Moore cemented the details of the Santa story, artist Thomas Nast created the definitive image of the modern Santa Claus—the smiling

Nast captured every element of the Santa story in his work, including the flying reindeer.

19

face, the apple-red cheeks and his white beard and plump figure. Nast, the head illustrator at *Harper's Weekly* for 30 years, created numerous drawings of Santa. In the process, he elaborated on details of the Santa story, establishing the North Pole as Santa's home and portraying him as a toymaker who was assisted by a workshop full of elves. Nast's pictures also depict other classic details: Santa checking his book to keep track of who's been naughty and who's been nice; kids sitting on his lap; Santa reading children's letters.

One of Nast's earliest, and most memorable, images was of Santa in a Union Army camp during the Civil War. Wearing a stocking cap and a fur-trimmed jacket decorated with stars (which would soon disappear), Santa distributes gifts (including copies of *Harper's Weekly*, the magazine the image appeared in) to the troops.

Santa as *Saturday Evening Post* Cover Boy

For the first half of the 20th century, *The Saturday Evening Post* was an influential magazine with one of the largest weekly circulations in America. Artists J.C. Leyendecker and Norman Rockwell's Santa cover art for the magazine continued Nast's earlier visions, portraying Santa toiling away with the elves to build toys, listening to a kid's wish list, stooping to hug a child despite the heavy sack of toys on his back, and plotting his Christmas Eve route on a globe.

Leyendecker's December 7, 1912, cover would nod to another developing Santa tradition: the ubiquity of the bell-ringing Salvation Army Santas who have become synonymous with the Christmas season today. To commemorate the death of Salvation Army founder William Booth earlier that year, Leyendecker's image depicted a Salvation Army Santa seemingly so grief-stricken by Booth's passing that he leans on a brick post for support.

Things Go Better with Santa

Santa's promotional power was verified once and for all with Haddon Sundblom's series of Christmas-themed ad campaigns for Coca-Cola,

Sparkling Holidays Forever stamps, first released in 2018, feature close-ups of Santa Claus from paintings by Haddon Sundblom.

from 1931 to 1964. His Santa is a friendly, jovial, hardworking figure, who takes a break from his toils to enjoy a refreshing Coke. Besides being used for ads, Sundblom's Santas were adapted for use on billboards, store displays, posters and dolls. And his original works are on display in museums across the country.

Today, Santa is a more potent marketing figure than ever who starts to appear everywhere, it seems, around the Fourth of July. He stars in ads for everything from the expected (Pillsbury, Coca-Cola, M&M's, Denny's) to the modern (Apple, Air New Zealand, Audi) to the unexpected (the NBA, Tide To Go pens, even Poo-Pourri air freshener). Although complaints about the commercialization of Christmas are voiced each year, an editorial first published in the *New York Sun* in 1897 sums up the icon's timeless appeal: "Yes, Virginia, there is a Santa Claus. He exists as certainly as love and generosity and devotion exist, and you know that they abound and give to your life its highest beauty and joy."

Coca-Cola has been using Santa in ads since the 1920s.

An illustration of *Lill's Travels in Santa Claus Land and Other Stories,* originally published in 1878, offers an early glimpse of Mrs. Claus.

MEET MRS. CLAUS

SANTA'S WIFE ENTERS THE LEGEND.

Mrs. Claus knows what Santa needs to get through the lengthy naughty and nice list.

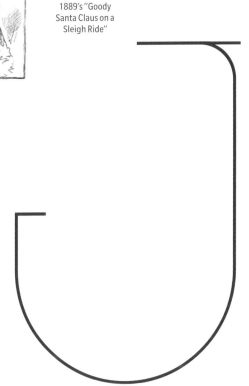

An illustration from 1889's "Goody Santa Claus on a Sleigh Ride"

SHAKE THE PACK!

Just who is Mrs. Claus? Is she the white-haired lady, a bit round like her husband, who stays home at the North Pole baking cookies and mending socks while her husband travels the world, as in such TV classics as *Rudolph the Red-Nosed Reindeer* (1964) or *Rudolph and Frosty's Christmas in July* (1979)? Or is she the budding feminist of poet Katherine Lee Bates' 1889 "Goody Santa Claus on a Sleigh Ride," in which, tired of Santa getting all the "glory" while she gets "nothing but the work," she demands equal rights? It turns out that, like most women, Mrs. Claus is all of these things, and more.

Though her birth origins remain murky, she may have hailed from the toyless Sombertown, ruled by the grouchy Burgermeister Meisterburger, as we learn in 1970's stop-motion TV special, *Santa Claus Is Comin' to Town*. Here, she's known as Jessica, and works as a schoolteacher, when she catches a youthful Kris Kringle handing out illicit toys. Still, he's able to win her over with the gift of a China doll.

From some of her youthful appearances, we've learned that she's always had spirit. The first mention of Mrs. Claus appears in an 1849 tale written by a Philadelphia missionary. In "The Christmas Legend," author James Rees recounts the story of a poor family mourning the loss of their eldest daughter, who ran away with a disreputable man. One Christmas Eve, the family welcomes a weary old traveling couple, offering them bread and cheese and their best bed.

The next morning, the family discovers a profusion of gifts they believe were delivered by "old Santa Claus and his wife." Imagine their surprise when the gift-giving couple ditch their disguises and reveal themselves as the long-lost daughter and her newly rich husband! There's no mention of the name, but this would seem to be Mrs. Claus.

After their wedding, of which the date remains uncertain, Mrs. Claus gave up teaching but settled into her role as an executive assistant to her busy husband. Though most attention is paid to her significant other, Mrs. Claus makes a cameo in the

"It's not just presents, and you know it. What about all that Christmas spirit and goodwill?"

MRS. CLAUS, *THE YEAR WITHOUT A SANTA CLAUS*

A redhead when she was younger, *The Year Without a Santa Claus'* Mrs. Claus still has streaks.

English actress Imelda Staunton voices Margaret Claus in 2011's *Arthur Christmas.*

Oscar winner Mira Sorvino (with Will Sasso) took her turn as Santa's wife in 2012's *Finding Mrs. Claus*, a made-for-TV movie in which, after going through a rough patch, the North Pole's most famous couple renew their vows in Las Vegas—in front of an Elvis impersonator, of course!

Mrs. Santa Claus, starring Angela Lansbury, was the first made-for-TV original musical since Rodgers and Hammerstein's *Cinderella* in 1957. It first aired in 1996 and revolves around Mrs. Claus getting stranded in New York after taking her hubby's sleigh out for a ride.

Judy Cornwell stars opposite David Huddleston in 1985's *Santa Claus: The Movie*. A box-office bomb at the time, the film—which attempts to explain many of the mysteries surrounding the jolly old elf—now has a cult following.

Elizabeth Mitchell joined the *The Santa Clause* trilogy in the second film, 2002's *The Santa Clause 2*. Tim Allen stars as Scott Calvin, a man who becomes Santa (during the first film in 1994). In the second installment, he learns that he must marry in order to keep the job.

Goldie Hawn appears as Mrs. Claus in 2018's *The Christmas Chronicles* (and the 2020 sequel) opposite long-time love, Kurt Russell, who plays Santa.

Delta Burke starred as Mrs. Claus (with John Goodman as Santa) in the 2006 live-action remake of *The Year Without a Santa Claus.*

1878 children's book *Lill's Travels in Santa Claus Land and Other Stories,* by Ellis Towne, Sophie May and Ella Farman. Here a girl named Lill recounts to her little sister, Effie, meeting Santa in Santa Claus Land. She followed the big guy to his observatory, where she saw "a lady sitting by a golden desk, writing in a large book," as Santa peered through his telescope to see who was being naughty and nice.

"Presently he said to the lady, 'Put down a good mark for Sarah Buttermilk. I see she is trying to conquer her quick temper,'" Lill recalls. " 'Two bad ones for Isaac Clappertongue; he'll drive his mother to the insane asylum yet.' "

As Lill finishes her story, Effie "wished Lill had found out how many black marks she had, and whether that lady was Mrs. Santa Claus."

With heavy snow frequently preventing reporting from the North Pole, Mrs. Claus' middle years are a blur, but it seems she began to chafe under the isolation. Witness her appearance in "Goody Santa Claus" (Goody stands for goodwife), when she demands that her husband take her along on his annual ride, even persuading him to let her slide down a chimney to deliver gifts. "Would it be so shocking," she asks, "if your goody filled a stocking?" At the conclusion of the journey, she is "gladdest of the glad. I've had my own sweet will."

After several more years of baking cookies and seeing to the needs of her husband's staff of elves, she was feeling unappreciated. As depicted in 1996's TV musical *Mrs. Santa Claus,* (set in the year 1910) starring Angela Lansbury, Mrs. Claus decides again to take off in her husband's sleigh. When one of the reindeer becomes injured, she's stranded in New York City. Going by the name Mrs. North, she has an awakening, becoming an advocate for women's rights and child-labor reform in the toy industry. Of course, Santa misses her terribly, and she eventually returns home, where a chastened Santa expresses his newfound respect for all she does at the North Pole.

Whatever name Mrs. Claus chooses to adopt when she's out in the world—Anya, in 1985's *Santa Claus: The Movie*; Margaret, in the 2011 British animated film *Arthur Christmas*; or perhaps the most apt, Mary Christmas, from the 1992 special *It's Christmastime Again, Charlie Brown*—it seems she never loses the spirit of Christmas. And while she may not have liked the decidedly retro 20th-century depictions of her, she clearly holds a deep love for her husband. However she's seen, Mrs. Claus likely finds comfort in her complexity. And among the best gifts of any season is knowing yourself.

SANTA'S HELPERS

THE ELVES ARE AN INTEGRAL PART OF THE CHRISTMAS STORY.

Some say *Little Women* author Louisa May Alcott introduced the idea of Christmas elves in an 1850 book. But that book was never published.

Buddy (Will Ferrell) can't keep up with the real elves when it comes to making toys in *Elf*.

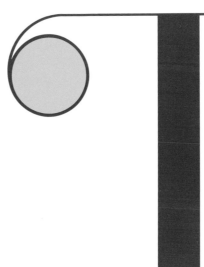T

Those toys don't make themselves! Santa Claus gets all the credit for delivering gifts to good boys and girls. But his workshop at the North Pole is staffed by an army of elves who toil year-round to make all those presents waiting under the tree.

Santa's little helpers are a later addition to the Christmas tale. Early depictions of Kris Kringle give elves short shrift. Though Clement C. Moore's 1823 poem, "A Visit from St. Nicholas," casts Santa as "a right jolly old elf," the verse makes no mention of his diminutive workers. Nor do the elves appear in Thomas Nast's iconic 19th-century illustrations of Santa Claus' toymaking enterprise.

Yet elves have been around even longer than Old St. Nick himself. Most scholars trace their origin to ancient Norse mythology. Magical beings, they were frequently seen as mischievous—and sometimes malevolent. In Scandinavian lore, for instance, the sprites were blamed for causing rashes and other diseases. Superstitious villagers would try to appease them by leaving out small gifts of butter.

Elves got an image makeover, thanks to a folktale collected by the Brothers Grimm, which shows the mythical creatures as hardworking and

Hermey the elf (below left) stars in *Rudolph the Red-Nosed Reindeer*.

helpful. In "The Elves and the Shoemaker," a poor cobbler gives away his last pair of shoes to a needy woman. He has just enough leather for one more pair. After cutting the leather to sew together the next day, he goes to bed. While he sleeps, elves arrive and stitch up the shoes, which the cobbler sells to buy more leather. Each night, the elves return to do their handiwork—until the shoemaker catches them in the act, and they disappear.

Christmas elves finally got their due in an 1857 poem published in *Harper's Weekly*. "The Wonders of Santa Claus" notes that Santa keeps a great many elves at work in his house upon a hill:

"All working with all their might,
To make a million pretty things,
Cakes, sugar-plums and toys,
To fill the stockings, hung up you know
By the little girls and boys"

By 1873, the notion that elves made Santa's toys was well-entrenched. *Godey's Lady's Book*, a precursor to today's women's magazines, published an illustration titled "The Workshop of Santa Claus." In it, Santa is surrounded by a collection of toys and elves. The caption reads: "Here, we have an idea of the preparations that are made to supply the young folks with toys at Christmastime."

THE MISCHIEVOUS 13

An ancient tradition in Iceland centers around the Yule Lads, 13 elves—one for each of the 13 days leading up to Christmas—with names like Sheep-Cote Clod (bothers the sheep), Stubby (steals leftover food from frying pans), Door Slammer (creates a racket in the middle of the night), Sausage Swiper (sneaks in the house to steal his favorite meat), and Spoon Licker (you guessed it, he licks your spoons). On each of the 13 nights, Icelandic children leave their shoes out in a conspicuous spot in the hopes they will receive a gift from that evening's visiting elf. If they've been good boys and girls, they will receive candy. For the naughty, it's rotting potatoes!

The Kringle family of elves takes in an abandoned baby in *Santa Claus Is Comin' to Town*.

"We elves try to stick to the four main food groups: candy, candy canes, candy corns and syrup." BUDDY, *ELF*

Elves Save the Day

More recently, Santa's elves have become an integral part of the Christmas legend. They are the man in red's assistants, cheerfully crafting toys for his annual journey. And some big- and small-screen representations give the tiny toymakers their due, demonstrating how frequently they are called upon to save Christmas.

Who can forget Hermey? In the 1964 stop-motion TV classic *Rudolph the Red-Nosed Reindeer*, the elf is a misfit, stuck in the workshop, but he dreams of becoming a dentist. Feeling similarly outcast, Hermey runs away with Rudolph but eventually saves the day with dentistry—pulling the teeth of the menacing Abominable Snow Monster.

Elves Jingle and Jangle also save Christmas in the 1974 TV special *The Year Without a Santa Claus*. A dispirited Santa wakes up with a cold and decides to cancel the holiday. Distraught, Mrs. Claus sends the pair to find proof that people still care about Christmas. Luckily, they succeed. And, when Santa passes over little Timmy's house on Christmas Eve in the 2009 TV special *Prep & Landing*, it's elves Wayne and Lanny who convince him to go back.

Several live-action elves have captured hearts, too. Dudley Moore played Patch, a rogue elf in the 1985 film *Santa Claus: The Movie*. Competing for the spot of top toymaker, Patch invents a machine to speed up production. And a generation of tween girls crushed on Bernard, David Krumholtz' head elf in the 1994 movie *The Santa Clause*, in which he whipped accidental Santa Tim Allen into shape. But the most beloved elf may be Will Ferrell's Buddy in 2003's heartwarming film *Elf*. A human raised by elves at the North Pole, Buddy sets out on a quest to find his birth father. Along the way, he discovers his own value in reviving the spirit of Christmas and helping power Santa's sleigh.

All these elves prove the maxim: Often the best things come in small packages.

Bernard (David Krumholtz) tells Scott (Tim Allen) that he must take over Santa's duties in *The Santa Clause*.

Godey's Lady's Book showed elves as industrious toymakers.

In *Prep & Landing*, a 2009 computer-animated TV special, it's elves Wayne and Lanny's job to get homes ready for Santa's arrival.

Who says elves aren't sexy? Elizabeth Banks plays blond elf Charlene in 2007's *Fred Claus*. She draws the attention of Santa's black-sheep older brother (Vince Vaughn), who helps out with Christmas because he's strapped for cash.

The reindeer names Donner and Blitzen mean "thunder" and "lightning" in German.

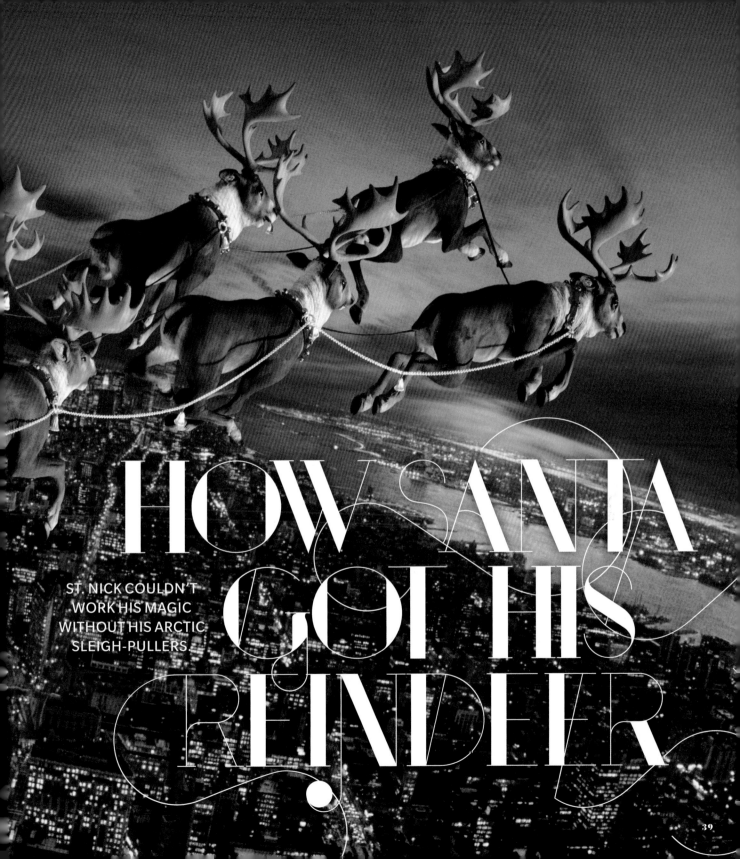

HOW SANTA GOT HIS REINDEER

ST. NICK COULDN'T
WORK HIS MAGIC
WITHOUT HIS ARCTIC
SLEIGH-PULLERS.

Reindeer comes from the Old Norse word *hreinn*, which means "horned animal."

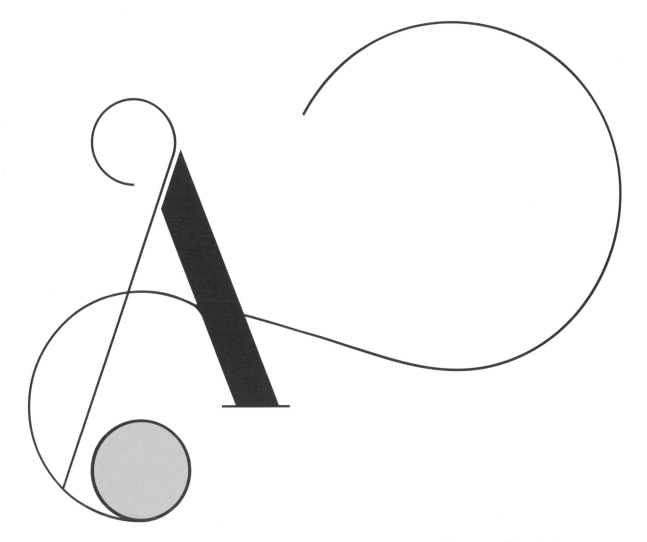

As he travels the world delivering toys on Christmas Eve, Santa Claus depends on eight tiny reindeer to pull his sleigh. It makes sense: The animals are native to the Arctic and subarctic regions of Northern Europe and Asia as well as North America, so Santa wouldn't have to travel far to round up a herd. Magically, his unusual steeds can fly, churning the air with their fur-covered hooves.

But Santa started with just one animal. An obscure illustrated children's poem appears to be the first work to depict Santa's reindeer-powered sleigh (see photo, page 42). Published in 1821, "Old Santeclaus with Much Delight," part of a small paperback volume called *The Children's Friend: A New-Year's Present to Little Ones from*

Five to Twelve, shows Santa being towed by a single antlered critter, along with the verse:

> *"Old SANTECLAUS with much*
>   *delight*
> *His reindeer drives this frosty night,*
> *O'r chimney tops, and tracts of snow,*
> *To bring his yearly gifts to you."*

Some other aspects of the Santa tradition are also in flux in the poem. A slim Santa wears a fur hat and, in one panel, he has a green suit.

Two years later, Clement C. Moore's "A Visit from St. Nicholas" (also known as "The Night Before Christmas") provided the definitive vision of Santa and his four-legged friends, upping the

Art for an 1821 poem depicted Santa's sleigh pulled by just one reindeer.

In L. Frank Baum's 1902 book, Santa is assisted by reindeer Glossie and Flossie, among others.

Only female reindeer keep their antlers during winter.

number to eight and even giving names to the reindeer:

> *"More rapid than eagles his coursers*
> *they came,*
> *And he whistled, and shouted, and called*
> *them by name:*
> *'Now, Dasher! Now, Dancer!*
> *Now, Prancer and Vixen!*
> *On, Comet! On, Cupid! On, Dunder and Blixen!*
> *To the top of the porch!*
> *To the top of the wall!*
> *Now dash away! Dash away!*
> *Dash away all!'"*

(The last two reindeer's names changed over time to Donner and Blitzen.)

Moore's version was not without its challengers. In the 1902 book, *The Life and Adventures of Santa Claus*, L. Frank Baum, the author of *The Wonderful Wizard of Oz*, packed his novel with a host of mythic beings, all fighting over the fate of Christmas. In this tale, Santa has 10 reindeer: Flossie and Glossie, Racer and Pacer, Fearless and Peerless, Ready and Steady, and Reckless and Speckless. The novel, in which a baby Santa is adopted by the Master Woodsman of the World and grows up to invent toys, failed to capture the public's imagination.

A more business-motivated image of Santa's reindeer did grab hold. In 1898, a missionary

SANTA'S SLEIGH MUST BE FUELED BY GIRL POWER

In *Rudolph the Red-Nosed Reindeer*, Donner is Rudolph's father. But now science proves that's not really possible. Male reindeer lose their antlers by mid-December. Only female reindeer have antlers at Christmastime. "Being members of the deer family, the males grow their antlers a little bit earlier—and just after mating season, they drop off. So over the winter, you'll never see a male with antlers," explained Andrew Hebda, a zoologist at Canada's Nova Scotia Museum.

successfully lobbied to import 600 reindeer from Siberia to help feed starving Inuit people in Alaska. Seeing a business opportunity, by 1926, Carl Lomen wanted to corner the market on reindeer meat, thinking it could rival beef. He, along with Macy's, conceived of a promotional parade led by Santa and his reindeer. Other towns followed suit with similar parades and the tradition stuck. (Lomen became known as the "Reindeer King," despite the meat never taking off in the United States.)

A new reindeer joined Santa's herd in 1939 in yet another marketing ploy, and he became the most famous reindeer of all: Rudolph, whose red nose guided Santa's sleigh on its rounds one foggy Christmas Eve. Rudolph was born when Robert May penned some verse for a booklet distributed to children in Montgomery Ward department stores. In May's tale, Santa visits Rudolph's home to deliver gifts on that murky night and recruits Rudolph on the spot to help him with his deliveries.

A decade later, country singer Gene Autry recorded a song about Rudolph written by May's brother-in law Johnny Marks, and it sold 1.75 million copies its first Christmas season. But it was the Rankin/Bass–produced classic *Rudolph the Red-Nosed Reindeer* that really made Rudolph an indelible part of Christmas. Reprised every year since its 1964 debut, the stop-motion TV special follows the adventures of Rudolph as he's teased for his unusual proboscis and runs away. After tangling with the Abominable Snow Monster, Rudolph returns to save Christmas, leading Santa's sleigh through the foggy night.

But not all reindeer are heroic. In the 1979 novelty hit, "Grandma Got Run Over by a Reindeer," a tipsy senior citizen is trampled by Santa's charges. Written by Randy Brooks and recorded by bluegrass musicians Elmo and Patsy, it's sold over 11 million copies and was made into a 2000 animated TV special. A radio mainstay during the holiday season, it nonetheless appears on many a "Worst Holiday Song" list. Still, as Elmo once said, "A lot of people say it's not really Christmas until they hear it."

Twenty-five years before he was on TV, Rudolph was the star of a booklet created for Montgomery Ward department stores.

Comet eats so much candy in *The Santa Clause 2* that he can't move, much less fly.

43

MYSTERY SOLVED

HOW DOES SANTA GET TO EVERYONE'S HOUSE TO
DELIVER PRESENTS IN JUST ONE NIGHT? A COMBINATION
OF SMART PLANNING, QUANTUM PHYSICS AND MAGIC!

To most, it may seem virtually impossible for one man to fly around the world on a sleigh, delivering Christmas presents to millions of children in one night—but Santa Claus is clearly not your average mortal. There are a number of factors, including science as well as a little magic, that help Father Christmas pull off his most extraordinary feat every December 24—and just in the nick of time.

With only a matter of hours to slide down millions of chimneys, time is of the essence for Santa. And luckily, it's on his side. Thanks to the planet's time zones, he's able to be one step ahead. He begins his journey at the International Date Line, near Eastern Russia and travels west, following the Earth's rotation around the sun, which helps him gain necessary extra time, so he actually has 32 hours to carry out his special operation.

In order to hit all 300 million homes of children who celebrate Christmas, Santa's sleigh must travel at an extraordinary rate of speed. How fast are we talking? *Nova*, the PBS science documentary series, spoke with experts who crunched the head-spinning numbers. First, there's the matter of distance. Although the global scale is more than 300 million waypoints, Santa's able to skip the ocean, desert and wilderness, leaving him fewer waypoints and only 3 million miles of ground to cover. Presuming he spends half of his 32 hours up in the sky and the other half delivering presents, his sleigh travels 3 million miles in 16 hours—or 187,500 miles per hour. That would explain why if you blink, you miss him. "That is quite a lot slower than the speed of light," explains Hannah Fry, a mathematician at University College London, "but substantially more than the speed of sound." So then how does he not create a sonic boom? Seems it's a silent night only Saint Nick could explain!

Another trick Santa has up his sleeve: Dasher, Dancer, Prancer, Vixen, Comet, Cupid, Donner and Blitzen (plus Rudolph, if it's a foggy night). According to Ian Stewart, a mathematics professor at Warwick University in England, they are Mr. Claus' secret weapon to pulling off his annual mission impossible. "Reindeer have a curious arrangement of gadgetry on top of their heads, which we call antlers and naively assume exist for the males to do battle and to win females. This is absolute nonsense. The antlers are actually fractal-vortex-shedding devices. We are talking not aerodynamics here, but antlaerodynamics."

And it seems Santa will only improve his game over time. Roger Highfield, author of *Can Reindeer Fly? The Science of Christmas*, speculates that somewhere at the North Pole "there must be an army of scientists experimenting with the latest in high-temperature materials, genetic computing technologies and warped spacetime geometries, all united by a single purpose: making millions of children happy, each and every Christmas."

TRACKING BIG RED

Thanks to a serendipitous mistake 61 years ago, children around the world know precisely when to expect the pitter-patter of hooves on their roof. As the legend goes, in December 1955, Sears Roebuck placed an ad in a Colorado Springs newspaper, encouraging youngsters to call Santa. But the number provided was one numeral off, and coincidentally sent all inquiries to the infamous red phone at the Continental Air Defense Command (CONAD) Operations Center—a phone that was reserved for urgent calls from the Pentagon.

As the calls came rolling in, Colonel Harry Shoup played along, replying with a jovial "Ho, ho, ho!" and revealing his whereabouts. Decades later, every Christmas, NORAD fields 100,000 calls— in addition to thousands of emails—asking about the current location of Santa's sleigh. Thanks to technology, fans can now also track him as early as December 1 at *noradsanta.org* and at *santatracker.google.com*.

A Merry Christmas

The image of Santa and his reindeer sleigh really took hold with 1823's "A Visit from St. Nicholas."

SURE, SANTA'S SLEIGH IS SUPREME, BUT CHECK OUT THESE OTHER WAYS THE GIFT-GIVER HAS TROTTED THE GLOBE.

HO, HO, HO, HE'S ON THE

A merry Christmas

In French history, St. Nick rode a donkey named Gui, which means "mistletoe."

Kris Kringle needed a wagon in the old days when the Yule log was the whole tree!

The yule goat comes from Scandinavia's holiday traditions!

Starting in 1925, the Goodyear Blimp spread holiday cheer, often with Santa along for the ride.

CHRISTMAS GREETINGS

Americans can't resist Father Christmas in a car!

GO, GO, GO!

47

CHAPTER 2

CLAUS-iAN CUSTOMS

FROM COOKIES TO CARDS AND CHRISTMAS TREES,
HOW OUR FAVORITE FESTIVE TRADITIONS CAME TO BE

When a home has a wood or coal stove instead of a fireplace, Santa still doesn't use the door: He squeezes through the stovepipe instead!

Santa was often depicted as miniature, or as an elf, to explain how he fit in chimneys.

WHY SANTA

DODGES THE FRONT DOOR

It turns out Santa wasn't the first to prefer the flue to the front door. Throughout time, the fireplace has long been a spot that drew magical visitors—fairies, witches and elves who were thought to enter through the chimney. In European frescoes dating back to the 14th century, St. Nicholas is seen dropping gold down chimneys. And two centuries later, Dutch children would leave their shoes by the fireplace the night before the Feast of St. Nicholas and wake to find them filled with candy and presents.

Washington Irving is thought to be the first to depict Santa using a stealth rooftop entry. In his 1809 *Knickerbocker's History of New York* he wrote St. Nick "rattles down the chimneys" one night annually. But it was really Clement C. Moore's 1823 "A Visit from St. Nicholas" that cemented the idea of the Big Guy arriving "Down the chimney...with a bound!" Skeptical about how the portly present-giver can fit? The explanation is simple: All it takes is a little bit of Christmas magic.

By 1867, the image of Santa on the roof had become part of his lore.

Illustrator Thomas Nast also depicted Santa going down the chimney in 1874.

KRISS KRINGLE MARCH

GEO. E. FAWCETTE
PHILADELPHIA.

HARPER'S WEEKLY
JOURNAL OF CIVILIZATION

DEAR SANTA

LEARN HOW AN ILLUSTRATOR AND A BURGEONING POST OFFICE HELPED GIVE CHILDREN A DIRECT LINE TO ST. NICK OVER 160 YEARS AGO.

Thomas Nast depicted the popularity of mailing letters to Santa as the trend picked up in the late 19th century.

Thomas Nast's Santa illustrations in *Harper's Weekly*, especially this one from 1871 featuring St. Nick sorting his mail, led to a boom in letters addressed to the North Pole.

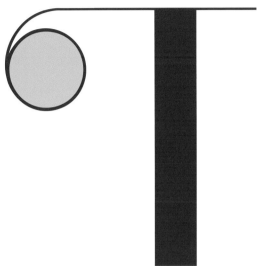

Until 1913, when the Postmaster General made an exception for letters addressed to Santa Claus, opening his mail or responding to the letters was technically illegal!

> "I'm sending a letter to Santa Claus/ My letter I hope he'll receive/ Oh, I wonder if he will please remember me/ When he calls on Christmas Eve."
>
> VERA LYNN, "I'M SENDING A LETTER TO SANTA CLAUS" (1939)

To a child, there are few tasks each year more important than crafting the perfect Letter to Santa. The message—usually a progress report highlighting yearly accomplishments to justify the subsequent Christmas Day wish list—is a delicate art. It's a lesson in correspondence (don't forget your greeting or your signature), prioritization (choose only the gifts you'd like most), and tact (don't be greedy).

The practice dates back nearly 150 years, when Santa himself would leave letters for young children—usually on the fireplace mantel— detailing behavior to improve upon in the coming year. Eventually, kids began to write back. After the Civil War, Americans were coming around to a new hand-delivered mail system, and children saw their postman as a conduit to Kris Kringle, especially after Thomas Nast's jovial depictions of Santa became an annual tradition in the pages of *Harper's Weekly*. National magazines and newspapers began to run stories featuring letters sent to local post offices, destined for the North Pole. The media attention and a nationwide acceptance of the USPS stamp system led to the practice becoming as common as it is today.

SANTA CLAUS
THE NORTH POLE

POSTAGE PAID
PB555330

Dear Santa Claus,

My name is Hannah   And I have been very good this year.
I hope that you are ok. My brother has been ok, and Mel too. My
mom has been bad all year. She goes to Bingo every week. I do not
like it at all. But she does win sometimes and buys us some things.
I hope that you and Mrs. Claus are ok. I would like a Easy Bake
Oven, Mermaid Barbie, Backpack Baby Doll, Games and Books.
Also a GIGA PET. Dress shoes(size 11 1/2). New Dresses. I hope to
get all of this. I hope that it really snows on Christmas Eve. I also
hope that Rudolph and all the other reindeer have been good for you.
Do you know all the kids? How do you get the toys that people make
for you? Do you go and get them, or do they bring them to you? Can I
stay up and see you when you come to my house? Would you like
milk and cookies? Do you want some carrots for the reindeer? My
dad has been good all year and helps my mom all the time. Would you
please bring something for Blaze and Ebony. Goodbye. I will talk to
you on Christmas Eve. if you let me stay up. PLEASE//////////////

XOXOXOXOXOXOXOXOXOXOXOXOXOXOXOXOXOXOXOXOX

LOVE
HANNAH
P.S. Tell Rudolph I said hi..

Dear, Santa
I want A trip to pennelvania
by myself with my very own ticket,
And A Lamborghini remote control not attached,
A tape cassete called cocktail,
My very own set of weights,
A poster of Michagan Wolvariens,
A Leather ~~girl~~ jacket with a eagle on
the back, Like I saw at Diarcys,
A set of oncitLapedias,
And Lots of surprizes, And have been very
                                      good.
from,
Trenton

Dear, Santa

This year I have been a very
good boy. I just wanted to ask how
the reindeer and elve's doing? And, also,
how do you get in my house? We dont
have a real chimney and we keep our
fireplace doors locked at night. Our fireplace
runs on gas, and at first I thought
it would make smoke and set off the
smoke alarm, like my sister and her friend
did when they lit to many scented candels...
I will give you my christmas list soon,
and most of the things on my list are
Minecraft stuff but i'm not sure if
you know what "Minecraft" is but you
probley will.

sincetly,
Blake

Dear
Santa   12-3-94
              I hope you come to
my house this year because you
forgot last year and I was sad
because I didn't get a present from
you. Well if you do come I wish
for clot of toys but I know I
could only ask for a couple because
theres other children who want
gifts to I will leave you
two cookies and a glass of
fresh milk ok I Love you
Santa heres my little list
                                I was a
                                very good girl

a barbie jeep
Telephone Tammy
a big bag of Gummy Bears   thats all
Happyness for everyone   Santa

write back
soon. your   By now
letter will be
the best gift   Angel
I can recieve.

I ♡ you
SANTA CLaus

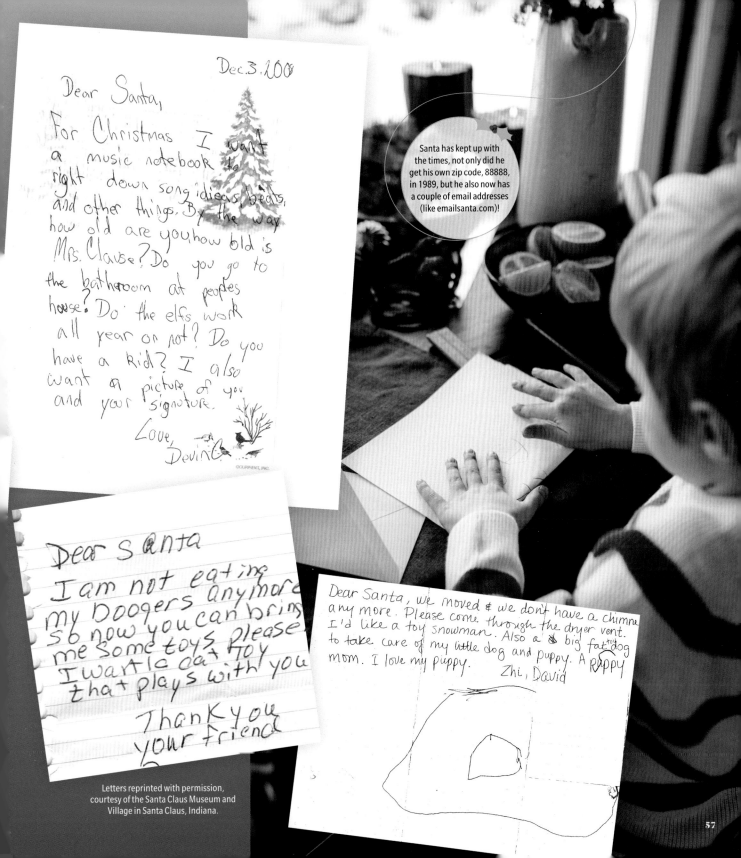

Dec. 3. 200

Dear Santa,
For Christmas I want
a music notebook to
right down song ideas, beats,
and other things. By the way
how old are you. how old is
Mrs. Clause? Do you go to
the bathroom at peoples
house? Do the elfs work
all year or not? Do you
have a kid? I also
want a picture of you
and your signoture.
Love,
Devin C.

©CURRENT, INC.

Santa has kept up with
the times, not only did he
get his own zip code, 88888,
in 1989, but he also now has
a couple of email addresses
(like emailsanta.com)!

Dear Santa
I am not eating
my boogers anymore
so now you can bring
me some toys please.
I want a cat toy
that plays with you

Thank you
your friend

Dear Santa, we moved & we don't have a chimney
any more. Please come through the dryer vent.
I'd like a toy snowman. Also a big fat toy dog
to take care of my little dog and puppy. A puppy
mom. I love my puppy.
Zhi, David

57

In 2020, Santa Claus will ride in on his sleigh as the final celebrity of the parade for the 94th time. He led the parade only once—back in 1933!

In the parade's second year, 1925, throngs of onlookers welcomed Santa's arrival on a horse-drawn float.

In 1939, a 57-foot Santa balloon became part of the parade. Three years later, the balloon collapsed and was retired.

POMP & CIRCUMSTANCE FOR
ST. NICK

SINCE 1924, SANTA'S APPEARANCE AT THE MACY'S THANKSGIVING DAY PARADE HAS MARKED THE START OF THE HOLIDAY SEASON. (CAN SOMEONE LET THE DEPARTMENT STORES AND RADIO STATIONS KNOW THAT?)

Each year, the Christmas hype seems to start earlier. Stores crank carols before Halloween, and enthusiastic early birds light their artificial trees before the first frost. But for Christmas purists in the United States, Santa's appearance in the Macy's Thanksgiving Day Parade has marked the true start to the season for the better part of a century.

Santa has been riding in to New York City's Herald Square on his signature float since the parade's inaugural year, 1924. Each Thanksgiving (except for one), he arrives last, ringing in the season before taking his post in the flagship store's eighth-floor Santaland.

In the parade's first year, 250,000 people lined the streets to watch Macy's employees in vibrant costumes, Central Park Zoo animals, marching bands and festive floats. But it was the 1947 movie *Miracle on 34th Street* that took the event to new heights. For the first time, the entire country caught a peek at the fanfare in the Big Apple, and were so enthralled that the following year the parade was broadcast live on NBC, a tradition that continues today.

One Santa proved he could fill a tall order when he walked on stilts in 1949.

STUFFED STOCKINGS

THE LEGEND MAY HAVE ORIGINATED
NEARLY 2,000 YEARS AGO, BUT SOCKS
OF ALL KINDS REMAIN AN INDISPENSABLE
PART OF OUR HOLIDAY TRADITION.

This 19th-century postcard
showed some lucky children
and a very large stocking!

In the mid-1800s, Christmas trees briefly supplanted stockings as the place where presents were left, but the stocking tradition made a comeback.

In 1986's *Jiminy Cricket's Christmas,* the whole Disney gang stuffed the stockings.

America's Sweetheart Shirley Temple got into the spirit in 1938.

"The stockings were hung by the chimney with care in hopes that St. Nicholas soon would be there."

"A VISIT FROM ST. NICHOLAS"

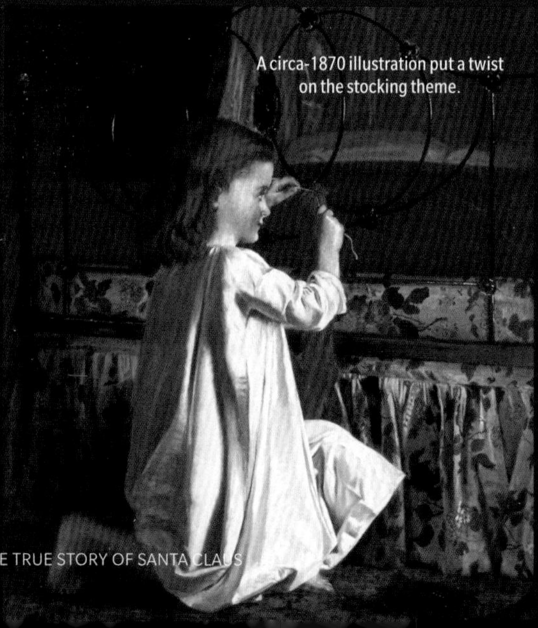

A circa-1870 illustration put a twist on the stocking theme.

Chew

WRIGLEY'S SPEARMINT CHEWING GUM

5ᵈ PER PACKET

Enjoy a Christmas treat—chew Wrigley's Spearmint Chewing Gum. Pop some in Christmas stockings too!

Healthful · Refreshing · Delicious

A 1956 Wrigley's ad promoted the idea of adding packs of gum to the Christmas stocking.

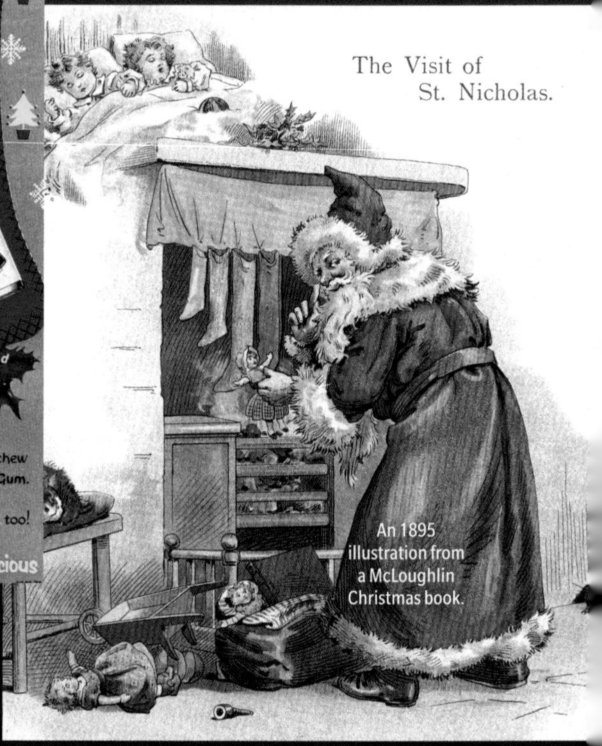

The Visit of St. Nicholas.

An 1895 illustration from a McLoughlin Christmas book.

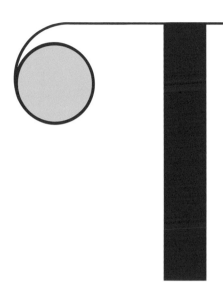

T

This tradition can be traced directly back to the St. Nicholas himself. As the story goes, there was once a very poor father who had three beautiful daughters. The father was distraught, as he had nothing to offer as a dowry, and so he knew his children were destined for dreary futures. When St. Nicholas caught wind of the father's predicament, he was determined to help, but knew the man was too proud to accept a gift. Instead, St. Nicholas climbed to the roof of the family's house in the night, slipping a bag of gold down the chimney (or through the window according to some versions) before they woke.

At the foot of the chimney, the three daughters had hung their stockings to dry by the heat of the fire. Imagine their surprise when, the next morning, each found a sack of gold coins—plenty of money for a generous dowry—in their socks. From that day forward, villagers would hang their stockings by the hearth, hoping a similar fortune would fall upon them.

Some think the tradition goes back even farther, to the Norse god Odin, who rode his eight-legged horse during the Yule season and children would leave sugar, carrots and hay for the horse and receive gifts in return.

Whatever the true story, hanging stockings with care has become a beloved, bountiful tradition.

Be Good for Goodness' Sake!

The rules are simple: If a child can't be bothered to stay on the Nice List, Santa doesn't bother himself with packing a present. Instead, naughty children are left only coal—easily accessible for a man who enters houses via chimney.

Of course, Santa took his inspiration from some mythical predecessors: St. Nicholas, the Netherlands' Sinterklaas and Italy's La Befana—a witch who flies on a broomstick—were all known to leave coal alongside other unpleasantries (think garlic, onions and twigs).

While the punitive move may seem out of character for the benevolent Santa Claus we know today, consider that his contemporaries tend to pair up with far more sinister disciplinarians to do their Naughty List bidding—Austria's Krampus, France's Père Fouettard and Germany's Knecht Ruprecht also bring coal to ne'er-do-wells; but legend has it they pair the unwelcome gift with beatings (often, not so ironically, with a bag of ashes) and even kidnappings.

MERRY MEET

"I have never been able to understand why the great gentleman lives at the North Pole," the first department store Santa, James Edgar, once said. "He is so far away...only able to see the children one day a year. He should live closer to them."

& GREETS

A GENEROUS AND INGENIOUS STORE OWNER MADE DREAMS COME TRUE FOR MILLIONS OF CHILDREN.

Being a department store Santa is no easy job. Some greet more than 17,000 kids a season, and in big cities it can be twice that!.

In a 1969 episode of *The Brady Bunch*, Cindy asks Santa for a Christmas miracle: a cure for her mom's laryngitis so she can sing in church.

"I remember walking down an aisle, and all of a sudden, right in front of me, I saw Santa Claus. I couldn't believe my eyes.... It was a dream come true," a man that had been at Edgar's store as a boy said years later.

The author's children with Santa in 1999.

CRY BABIES

Walk into a shopping center this holiday season and you'll probably spot a winding queue of children dressed in their December best, waiting for a meeting with Mr. Claus. This practice began back in 1841, when one Philadelphia store decided to display a life-size model of Santa that children could visit. Thousands of boys and girls showed up for a glimpse of their holiday hero in person.

Still, it wasn't until 1890, after Santa's image had standardized into the jolly fat man in the red suit—an image due in part to Thomas Nast's popular illustrations in *Harper's Weekly*—that the first store Santa entered the scene.

To surprise the children in his Massachusetts dry goods store, James Edgar donned a Santa costume he had custom made in Boston and greeted shoppers with glee. Edgar took his job of giving seriously: The entrepreneur was known for helping to pay for children's medical care and offering jobs in his store to youths in need.

Edgar was just the first in a line of thousands of department store Santas, who've also earned their close-ups in film and TV. Whether the Santas are warm and wise, as in *Miracle on 34th Street*, or disappointingly parental (see: *A Christmas Story*), a visit with a department store Santa is a tradition no child wants to leave off the Christmas list.

Some parents think crying baby photos are cute, but department store Santas disagree. "The crying picture is not any fun for the kid and it's not any fun for Santa either," RG Holland told MentalFloss.com.

It's not crying children most mall Santas take issue with. One frustrated Kringle told MentalFloss.com, "Parents are the worst part of being Santa."

According to the National Christmas Tree Association, approximately 30 million Christmas trees are sold in the United States each year, making it a $1 billion industry!

O CHRISTMAS TREE

FROM THE MAJESTIC, TOWERING ROCKEFELLER CENTER STUNNER TO CHARLIE BROWN'S HUMBLE FIR, EVERGREENS HAVE LONG BEEN A PART OF THE MAGICAL SEASON.

Martin Luther (left), a 16th-century German preacher, is often credited as the first person to bring a Christmas tree indoors.

Queen Victoria, Prince Albert and their children (and tree) in 1848

Decking the halls, stringing popcorn, hanging candy canes— these are time-honored traditions to help make Christmas merry and bright. The sight (and scent, for some) of a trimmed tree on December 25, with presents from Santa stacked beneath, is the quintessential Christmas moment.

Many, many years before there were Christmas tree farms, winter greenery held a special place in ancient cultures. Common customs included bringing evergreen trees indoors to ward off evil spirits, bring good luck and celebrate the impending spring. Ancient Egyptians used the trees to honor the sun god Ra—believing the winter solstice would strengthen him. The Romans honored Saturn, God of Agriculture, with a midwinter feast called Saturnalia—trees and shrubs were brought inside, foreshadowing the bountiful farms of the future. The European Druids would decorate their temples with firs and pines to represent everlasting life.

This 1882 illustration shows how trees used to be decorated with toys.

Jackie Kennedy began the tradition of selecting a theme for the White House Christmas tree. In 1961, it was *The Nutcracker Suite*. The following year, shown here, she added ornaments made by disabled and senior citizens.

President John F. Kennedy and the First Lady pose in front of the White House tree in 1962.

FIRS, SPRUCES AND PINES, OH MY!

The perfect tree looks a little different to everyone. Though dozens of types of pine and evergreen trees find their way to Christmas tree farms each year, here are five classics to get you started.

Balsam Fir

Balsams give off the classic evergreen scent.

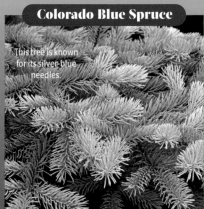

Colorado Blue Spruce

This tree is known for its silver-blue needles.

The very first Rockefeller Center Christmas Tree (1933) stood as a symbol of hope during the Depression. Today, it attracts 125 million people a year.

The first Christmas trees can be traced back to 16th-century Germany, when trees, or sometimes pyramid-shaped stacks of wood, were brought indoors and decorated to celebrate the season. The tradition remained largely in Europe, spreading from nation to nation and growing (preacher Martin Luther is believed to have started adding candles to the tree branches—in recognition of the stars in the night sky). In the United States, early Puritans distrusted the pagan tradition, and their rejection of the custom spilled into American Christianity until the 1840s. And while German settlements in Pennsylvania are

Douglas Fir

Pyramid-shaped Douglas Firs can grow up to 330 feet tall.

Fraser Fir

Their sturdy branches are perfect for heavy ornaments.

Scotch Pine

These needles range from blue-green to darker green.

White artificial trees, like this one Liz Taylor poses in front of, were popular in the 1950s.

Mickey's Christmas Carol

Charlie Brown's famous flimsy Christmas tree

The Bailey family decorates (while George sulks) in *It's a Wonderful Life*.

A runaway tree in *Christmas with the Kranks*

The Griswolds' uprooted tree in *National Lampoon's Christmas Vacation*

"I never thought it was such a bad little tree. It's not bad at all, really. Maybe it just needs a little love."

LINUS VAN PELT, *A CHARLIE BROWN CHRISTMAS*

believed to have had community Christmas trees dating as far back as 1747, the first record of a tree on display is not until 1830.

The tree tradition didn't truly catch on in the United States, however, until 1846, when sketches of England's Queen Victoria, Prince Albert and their family around their decorated tree appeared in the *Illustrated London News*. East Coast elites were eager to emulate the royals, and the Christmas tree rose to fame. Quickly, Americans had supersized the symbol of the season (European trees usually measured just 4 feet) and began placing them in town centers. And just like that, a once-rejected tradition became forevermore linked with the holiest of nights.

TREES

The Mount Ingino tree in Gubbio, Italy, stretches over 2,000 feet.

In a Rio de Janeiro lagoon, a 230-foot tree floats each season.

The tree in Tokyo Bay also boasts views of the Rainbow Bridge.

A holographic tree floats above visitors at the Rijksmuseum in Amsterdam.

Three hundred stalls pack around a tree at the Christmas market in Dortmund, Germany.

A giant tree is erected in the heart of Galeries Lafayette's central court in Paris.

In London, the tree at Claridge's is decorated by a renowned designer each year.

Artist Jim Pollack's Hubcap Tree stands in Baltimore, Maryland.

A glass tree is displayed on the Venetian island of Murano in Italy.

This tree of lights brightens Milan's Piazza del Duomo.

Over one million children send letters to Santa in the U.S. alone—imagine how much money he'd have to spend on stamps to send cards back to them all!

CHRISTMAS GREETINGS

OVER 2 BILLION HOLIDAY CARDS ARE SENT IN THE U.S. EACH YEAR.
HERE'S HOW THE TRADITION CAME TO BE, AND WHY IT'S STILL GOING STRONG.

The very first Christmas card, designed in 1843, caused a bit of controversy as it appears to show a child drinking some wine.

A jovial Santa circa 1900 sends Christmas wishes.

The holidays are a busy time for everyone—between tree trimming and festive fetes, the weeks between Thanksgiving and Christmas Day seem to melt away faster that Frosty in a greenhouse. As it turns out, seasonal stress may be a tradition as old as the Yuletide. A tradition not quite so ancient? Christmas cards. Today, their arrival may be as anticipated as that of Old St. Nick himself, but that wasn't always the case. The history of the greeting card begins in Britain in the early 1840s, when civil-servant and society snob, according to some, Sir Henry Cole was feeling the pressure of the "Christmas crunch," and created a time-saving solution to the stacks of customary Christmas letters that were collecting in his home. "In Victorian England, it was considered impolite not to answer mail," Ace Collins, author of *Stories Behind the Great Traditions of Christmas*, once said. "He had to figure out a way to respond to all of these people."

So Cole commissioned his friend, artist John Callcott Horsley, to design a seasonal card. Horsley's design showed three generations toasting to a Merry Christmas, flanked on each side by images of charity. At the top was a "To:_____." Now, Cole could simply address the cards he had printed and send them

77

Norman Rockwell designed 32 cards for Hallmark between 1948 and 1957, including "Santa Looking at Two Sleeping Children."

By 1878, Santa Claus was a Victorian Christmas superstar.

Early Christmas cards were 5 x 3 inches or smaller, or they were postcards.

Santa's mistletoe wreath symbolizes good luck and eternal love.

The Victorian Age placed the focus on family, as shown in this card.

Louis Prang's designs often incorporated natural elements, and fairy-tale fantasy-type images.

Many early cards depicted the Nativity scene, like this French one from 1900.

off, eschewing impoliteness in seconds. The idea took off, and by 1880, the industry had ballooned to more than 11.5 million Christmas cards per year.

Global Greetings

In 1876, Louis Prang, a Prussian who moved to Boston after the German Revolutions of 1848–49 failed, became known as the Father of the American Christmas card. Unlike his English predecessors, Prang's designs did not depict a festive scene. Instead, he focused on animals and nature. Six years later, Prang was printing 5 million cards a year— transitioning from natural motifs to more traditional designs like snowscapes and Santa Claus. He took pride in the artistic process and held competitions for well-known artists to design the next card. But in the early 1890s, inexpensive German-imported postcards flooded the market, knocking Prang and his opulent cards of silk and tassel out of the game.

When You Care Enough...

In 1915, Hall Brothers, a postcard printing company, gave Christmas cards a shot in an effort to save their struggling company. Clearly it worked—the company was later renamed Hallmark! Joyce, Rollie and William Hall developed the card format we know today: folded over and inserted into an envelope. "They discovered that people didn't have enough room to write everything they wanted to say on a postcard," said Steve Doyal, vice president of public affairs for Hallmark, "but they didn't want to write a whole letter."

Modern Mail

From pioneers like Cole and Prang to American visionaries like the Hall brothers to the thousands of designers today, this is a tradition that is poised to last. While snail mail has dropped dramatically in the advent of email and texting, greeting cards continue to thrive as younger generations embrace the industry. "It's not always the touchy-feely, 'to you and yours on this festive, glorious occasion' kind of prose," Peter Doherty, executive director of the Greeting Card Association, has said. "The newer publishers are writing in a language that is speaking to a younger generation."

BY THE NUMBERS When it comes to greeting cards, snail mail still reigns.

Over **2 billion** Christmas cards are sent in the U.S. each year.

61% of all seasonal greeting cards sent are Christmas cards.

A San Francisco man set a world record when he sent 62,824 Christmas cards in 1975.

Average price a family spends on Christmas cards **$29.14**

The average family receives **20** cards per year.

$28,158 Price of world's most expensive Christmas card, which sold at auction in 2001 to an anonymous buyer. It was one of the 1,000 lithographs made of the very first Christmas card in 1843.

Women buy 80% of all greeting cards.

SANTA

THROUGH THE

A MERRY CHRISTMAS

Boys

Girls

1910

A MERRY CHRISTMAS

Merry Christmas

1911

A MERRY CHRISTMAS

1914

A Merry Christmas

1915

Merry Christmas

1917

Just a little card ~ but ......
LOADS of Christmas Wishes

1925

Christmas Greetings ~ BROTHER

A simple Christmas greeting ~
Brother dear ~ just to express
The wish that Christmas brings you
Lots of cheer and happiness

1926

In this BAG
is something
just for You.
Merry Christmas

1927

HELLO THERE!

1929

YEARS

A LOOK AT HALLMARK CARDS OVER THE PAST CENTURY GIVES US A GLIMPSE AT ST. NICK'S EVOLUTION.

Forget to Remember
A Friend Like You?
Say "I couldn't if I would —
and
I wouldn't if I could!
MERRY CHRISTMAS

192

FOR A MERRY
CHRISTMAS

Christmas
Greetings

1931

for
YOU

SANTA'S
BACK
AGAIN!
Merry
Christmas

193

Merry Christmas
LITTLE FRIEND
Lots of Christmas wishes
And every single one
A wish that Christmas time will bring you
Lots and lots of fun

1933

HELLO
THERE!

193

1934

MERRY
CHRISTMAS   HAPPY
BIRTHDAY

This brings a "Happy Birthday"
With your Christmas wish — because
You weren't delivered by the stork —

19

Merry
Christmas!

1943

Hello!

19

Christmas
Greetings

1947

Christmas
Greetings

HOPE THESE WISHES
ARE AS WARM

19

81

SEASON'S GREETINGS

1949

FROM ANY POINT OF VIEW --

1953

1954

1956

Merry Christmas
Happy New Year

1958

1961

1962

1962

1967

NOEL
JOY NOEL
CHRISTMAS
GREETINGS
HOLIDAY
SEASON
MERRY
CHRISTMAS
HAPPY NEW
YEAR

1969

MERRY CHRISTMAS

1971

Merry Christmas

1972

1976

1977

1979

1980

1981

1981

1982

1986

1987

1993

1994

1995

1996

1998

2000

2001

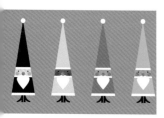

2005

2007

2009

2011

2012

2014

2015

2019

2019

COOKIES FOR KRINGLE

DISCOVER THE HARDY HISTORY OF SANTA CLAUS' CHRISTMAS EVE FUEL.

Christmas Greeting With love

Family cookie recipes are often passed down through generations.

It's Christmas Eve and the stage is set for Santa's arrival. The stockings are hung with care. The tree is glistening in lights. And the cookies are placed on a special plate with a cold glass of milk by its side. But wouldn't Santa be better off with an energy bar, or a strong cup of coffee? Maybe. But baking cookies for Christmas is a tradition that dates back to medieval times and isn't going to change anytime soon.

A Historical Hybrid

Modern cookie traditions can be linked to early winter solstice celebrations—when people prepared for the lean, cold months with festivals usually involving food. Eventually these customs merged to create our common practice.

In European pagan traditions, edible gifts were offered to spirits in exchange for a blessing, while in Norse mythology, children would leave hay for the god Odin's eight-legged horse, Sleipnir, during the Yuletide. In exchange, the god left treats.

In the Christian tradition, one theory traces back to the story of St. Nicholas himself. The fourth-century bishop was known for his generosity toward children and those in need. By the 16th century,

Santa takes in about 150 billion calories during his trek around the globe.

CONFECTIONS
AROUND THE WORLD

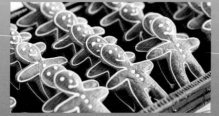

Made with ginger and sweetened with honey, gingerbread cookies are popular in the United Kingdom.

Fattigmann, knot-shaped, deep-fried cookies, are a holiday staple in Norway.

Pepparkakor are thin and spicy gingersnaps that Swedes can't get enough of.

Small round biscuits with nuts called pfeffernuss are enjoyed in Germany.

In Norway, sandbakelse—sugar cookies pressed in fluted tins—are customary.

In Germany and Austria, springerle biscuits are popular at Christmastime.

Santa loves Amish sugar cookies: simple wafers from Pennsylvania.

Dutch tots, too young to attend the grand feast celebrating St. Nick on December 6, would leave treats out for attendees. In the morning, the children would find their offerings exchanged for presents. Medieval German families would decorate a paradise tree—symbolic of the Garden of Eden—with apples and wafers, and Santa could grab a snack as he passed through. How could he resist? Pastries were changing as spices, like nutmeg and cinnamon, and exotic dried fruits became more widely available. As people transitioned from putting food on the tree (which attracted vermin) to glass ornaments, children set cookies out by the fire before bed, instead.

Victorian Values

One of the first American literary references to the milk-and-cookie tradition appears in the 1877 short story "Polly: A Before-Christmas Story." The timeline comes as no surprise, as hospitality was paramount to proper Victorian society. If one were hosting a visitor, it was common practice to leave out a snack. To convince children that, "Yes, Santa is real and is coming to our house tonight," parents chose cookies to welcome him.

The Role of the Great Depression

From the 1880s to the 1920s, a wave of European emigrants brought traditions to the United States that would shape today's culture. Not long after, the Great Depression hit. But instead of hoarding food to satiate their hungry stomachs, many parents instead took the opportunity to instill generosity in their children. The custom of leaving cookies for Santa, already circulating for decades, popularized as moms and dads used it to illustrate thankfulness.

Today's Treats

It's no wonder that Santa's belly still shakes like a bowl full of jelly—over one million households in the United States alone leave cookies out each Christmas Eve. In a world of fad diets and a shift toward clean eating, it seems the cookie custom is here to stay. And how sweet it is!

Goodies Galore

Santa is known to pack on the pounds, and this is why! Look at all these snacks left out for him every year.

Chile
Pan de Pascua, a sweet cake filled with fruit

Ireland
A pint of Guinness

Denmark
Risalamande, an almond rice pudding

France
A glass of wine

England
Sherry and mince pies made of dried fruit

Joulupukki, the Finnish Santa, is kind today—but he has a dark past.

GOING GLOBAL

Italy's Babbo Natale is thinner than Santas in other countries.

The name Santa Claus is derived from the Dutch Sinterklaas.

Sweden's Jultomten blends Santa and their folkloric gnomes.

WHETHER YOU CALL HIM PAPAI NOEL OR BABBO NATALE—
OR EVEN IF YOU ARE VISITED BY A MONK INSTEAD OF SANTA—
THE MESSAGE IS THE SAME: REMEMBER TO BE GOOD!

In Australia, Santa Claus poses on top of the famed Sydney Opera House overlooking the harbor to signal the start of the venue's Christmas season.

Brazil's Santa often wears a red silk cloak in the warm weather.

Father Christmas (here from Germany, circa 1925), takes on different looks around the world.

I

It's not just Santa Claus who delivers presents to good boys and girls. In Finland, the Yule Goat takes on gift-giving duty, Japan has a jolly Buddhist monk, and three kings do the job in Spain. Here, we go global for a roundup of the most fascinating Santa stories.

The "poop log" is a Christmastime tradition in Catalonia, Spain (see page 97).

Australia

Down Under, Santa Claus arrives in the middle of summer—leading the Aussies to rework many Western traditions to fit the season. In addition to changing the lyrics to the snowier carols, Santa also gets a style makeover and he's known to give his reindeer some well-deserved time off and ask kangaroos to guide his sleigh instead. While many Australians enjoy midday dinner on the beach, Santa can be spotted in his same red-and-white color scheme, but he tosses the fur collar, pants and boots in favor of shorts (and sometimes a swimsuit!)

Austria

St. Nicholas visits the good boys and girls of Austria on December 6, leaving them gifts. And children here have extra incentive to behave! St. Nick is often accompanied by Krampus, a horned monster meant to punish those who have been naughty. Some children also receive presents from the Christkind. For more on her, see Germany on page 93.

Brazil

December is summertime in Brazil, so "Papai Noel" (Papa Christmas), aka "Bom Velhinho" (Good Old Man), may wear a red silk robe. On Christmas Eve, children leave their socks near a window (there aren't many fireplaces in this tropical country), hoping they'll be full of presents come morning. Though Papai Noel is said to live in Greenland, he can be of any race, a reflection of Brazil's mixed African, European and indigenous heritage.

The Christkind opens the famous Christmas market in Nuremberg, Germany, each year on the Friday before the start of Advent.

The French Santa, Père Noël, wears a hood instead of a hat.

Joyeux Noël

China

Most Christmas traditions are Western imports in China (only 1 percent of the country is Christian; the holiday is mostly celebrated only in cities). Still, Santa Claus, called "Sheng dan Lao ren," or "Old Christmas Man," shows up in malls, often with female assistants, sometimes known as his sisters. For unknown reasons, the jolly elf often is portrayed playing the saxophone. As the holiday grows in popularity, it looks like this jazzy Santa is here to stay.

England

The U.K.'s Father Christmas is a kindly figure who brings presents to children, but he wears a long green robe and a wreath of ivy or mistletoe on his head—a nod to his roots in pagan mid-winter festivals when he reigned as King Winter. Before he got a G-rated makeover in the 19th century, however, Father Christmas was associated with delivering Christmas spirit rather than gifts, and encouraging people to eat, drink and be *very* merry.

Finland

Presents here are delivered by "Joulupukki," which means "Yule Goat." Adapted from an old Norse legend about an evil spirit who knocked on doors and demanded gifts and leftovers during the pagan mid-winter Yule festival, he's a man who's transformed into a goat on Christmas Eve.

In the late 1920s, thanks to popular radio programs, Joulupukki began taking on many of the same characteristics as Santa Claus. Since then, he's gone door to door on Christmas Eve (with a human chaperone); at every house, he asks, "Are there any well-behaved children here?" If the answer is yes, he hands over presents.

Many children believe Joulupukki lives in northern Finland's Lapland, north of the Arctic Circle. People around the world send more than 500,000 letters and cards to Santa Claus in Finland.

France

France's "Père Noël" or "Papa Noël" is much like Santa Claus, except he wears a long red cloak and carries his presents in a basket like the one used by grape pickers. On Christmas Eve, kids leave out their shoes as well as carrots for Père Noël's donkey, and if they have been good, he leaves them little presents—small toys, candy, money. If they've been bad, they may face a reckoning with Père Fouettard (Father Whip), who spanks naughty children.

Germany

Father Christmas ("der Weihnachtsmann") is the main gift-giver in Germany, delivering to children on December 24. In the southeastern parts of the country, an angelic girl called the Christ Child ("Christkind") brings presents. She has long blond hair, wears a white-and-gold gown and a crown, and

In earlier times, Santa was often shown wearing colors other than red.

exudes peace and serenity. Children write her letters asking for gifts and glue sugar to the envelopes to make them glisten. On Christmas Eve, some children hear a bell indicating the Christkind has decorated the tree and left presents. In some towns, a teenage girl is chosen to play the Christkind in the weeks before Christmas; children come to take pictures with her and tell her what gifts they want, just like a department store Santa. Still another visitor, St. Nicholas ("der Nikolaus") drops off small treats in shoes that German children have left by the door on the night of December 5.

Iceland

No Santas here. Instead there are 13 Yule Lads, who used to be known as mischievous pranksters but have recently rehabbed their image and are now known as benevolent gift-givers, similar to Santa.

Icelandic kids who don't get new clothes by Christmas Eve are told they'll be gobbled up by "Jólakötturinn" (the Yule Cat), a mythical beast who lives in the hills. The tradition is said to have originally been an incentive for farmworkers to finish processing the autumn wool before the holiday.

Ireland

Ireland's Santa-themed attractions put U.S. department store setups to shame. One mall in Dublin has a Santa Experience that includes a tour of an ersatz North Pole where kids can meet Santa, known as "San Nioclás" (St. Nicholas) or "Daidí na Nollag" (Father Christmas) and visit his house as well as the elves' post office, Santa's reindeer stable and the sleigh station. Other Santa lands are set up in castles, hotels, zoos, malls, even airports, where kids can ride on tractor pulls or take a train trip.

Italy

"Babbo Natale" (Father Christmas) brings gifts to children on Christmas, but they also receive them on the Epiphany (January 6) from a good witch known as "La Befana." According to legend, the Three Kings stopped at La Befana's house on their way to visit baby Jesus and invited her to join them. She demurred, but then changed her mind, filled a basket with gifts for Jesus, and tried to catch up with them on her broomstick. Now, the night before the Epiphany, she flies all over Italy, delivering gifts to the good children (and coal to the naughty ones). Today, many women in Italy dress up as La Befana to celebrate the Epiphany.

Japan

Even though fewer than 1 percent of Japanese are Christian, many have adapted Christmas

According to legend, Sinterklaas visits the Netherlands in December, but lives in Spain the rest of the year.

traditions—with a homegrown twist. Instead of Santa, there's a happy-go-lucky Buddhist monk named Hoteiosho, who also has a big belly and carries a sack of toys for good children on New Year's Eve. He is said to have eyes in the back of his head, so he can see who's being naughty or nice.

Don't expect a holiday ham or traditional turkey on the table in Japan. Fried chicken is the must-have meal. And not just any fried chicken—it has to be KFC. Millions of Japanese wait in hours-long lines or order their buckets in advance. According to the BBC, 3.6 million Japanese families eat the finger-lickin' good fast food during the Christmas season, thanks to clever marketing.

When the first KFC opened in Japan in 1970, the country did not have any established Christmas traditions. Manager Takeshi Okawara seized the opportunity with a promotion called "Kurisumasu ni wa Kentakkii" or Kentucky for Christmas.

The Netherlands

"Sinterklaas" is the Dutch version of St. Nicholas (one of the major inspirations for the modern Santa Claus; see page 10). Clad in a red robe, wearing a bishop's hat, and carrying a jeweled staff, Sinterklaas arrives by ship in mid-November. He mounts his white horse and parades through town. In the weeks leading up to his feast day on December 6, Sinterklaas appears in celebrations, visiting schools and shopping centers. On St. Nicholas Day, children put a carrot or some hay for Sinterklaas' horse in their wooden shoes and leave them out by the fireplace; in the morning they find the gifts he's left.

Nigeria

As in most former British colonies, Nigeria has Father Christmas. But he doesn't leave presents at children's houses—parents take them out to meet him at stores and shopping centers.

Russia

In a country where some towns average minus 58 degrees Fahrenheit during the winter months, it's fitting that the Russian Santa Claus is known as

Father Frost and his granddaughter, the Snow Maiden, stroll the streets of Sochi in western Russia.

JULTOMTEN
PRAKTUPPLAGAN · TIONDE ÅRGÅNGEN
1900

UTGIFVEN ⚬ AF ⚬ SVENSK ⚬ LÄRARETIDNING ⚬ STOCKHOLM

The Swedish Jultomten is an elf-like version of Santa (see page 97).

In Spain, Los Reyes Magos, the Three Kings, lead parades and bring children their gifts on the Feast of the Epiphany (January 6).

In Japan, fried chicken from Col. Sanders' KFC is often on the menu. In 2012, Japan Air Lines even offered a KFC two-piece chicken meal for travelers over the Christmas holiday!

"Ded Moroz," or Father Frost. Often accompanied by his granddaughter, a snow maiden named Snegurochka, Father Frost places presents under the New Year tree on New Year's Eve (a relic of the Soviet focus on secular holidays). Not unlike Santa Claus, Ded Moroz has a long white beard and is dressed for the weather, in a red or blue coat and tall "valenki" (felted boots). Rudolph doesn't guide Father Frost's "troika," or sleigh; instead, three horses drive him through the night.

Spain

Spanish niños receive small presents from Santa Claus on Christmas, but then get an even bigger haul on Epiphany (January 6) when "Los Reyes Magos," the Three Wise Men, arrive! Children write letters to their favorite king—Melchior, Gaspar or Balthasar—detailing their wish list. On January 5, the Kings ride in a huge parade. Boys and girls leave their shoes out, filled with sweets for the Wise Men and hay for their camels. The next day, they wake up early to discover the gifts the Magi have left.

In early December in the Catalonia region of Spain, kids get a "Tió de Nadal" (Christmas log), a special hollow log that they need to care for until Christmas. They "feed" the log and keep it warm. On Christmas, they sing special songs while beating the log with sticks, demanding that it "eliminate"— the log then poops nuts and candy, and eventually an onion or herring, the (smelly) sign the Tió de Nadal is empty!

Sweden

"Tomte" or "Jultomten," is an elf-like version of Santa from traditional Swedish folklore. On Christmas, a family member dresses up as Tomte, in a face mask and a red robe, and enters the house, asking, "Are there any good children here?" before distributing presents.

Back in the mid-1800s, no specific character was associated with the December gift-giving spree. Servants would flood the streets in full mask and costume, singing and exchanging presents with friends. Soon, specific characters began to crystallize, including the Christmas goat, called Julbocken, a 700-year-old hooved animal who left gifts for good children. Today, the character of Jultomten, a hybrid of St. Nicholas, Julbocken and a garden gnome, has largely taken the goat's place, but Swedish families continue to decorate their homes with the Yule Goat.

While it's Tomte who actually brings presents, the Yule Goat has remained a popular Christmas figure in Sweden. Giant straw statues of him have been erected in the small town of Gävle since 1966.

Switzerland

On December 6 (Saint Nicholas Day), the Swiss figure of "Samichlaus," rides in on his donkey, with a bag of treats like chocolate, nuts and mandarins, and dispensing advice to children who've been good. Next to him, you may also spot his sinister sidekick, Schmutzli, adorned in a spooky long black robe.

Legend of the Xmas Pickle

Back in the late 1840s, Germany began producing glass-blown ornaments, many in the shapes of fruits and vegetables. Woolworth stores began importing these baubles in 1880—around the same time the tale about the German tradition of the Christmas Pickle began to circulate. As the story goes, the pickle was to be the last ornament hung on the tree. The first child to find the cured cucumber ornament was to receive an extra present. "Nicht wahr," say the Germans. No such tradition exists there. Looks like the Woolworth Company had a pretty savvy marketing team!

Today, Schmutzli often plays a silent second fiddle to Santa, helping him distribute gifts, but traditionally, the character was not so jolly—he carried twigs to whip the boys and girls whose behavior warranted no treats, and was said to use the oversize treat bags to kidnap the bad children.

Ukraine

In Ukraine, a post-Soviet version of Russia's communist-era Father Frost has emerged as their gift-giving character. Ukrainian St. Nick ("Svyatyy Mykolay") wears a red bishop's robe and hat, and is often accompanied by an angel and devil, a stark reminder that children must be good and stay away from evil. Some lucky kids receive their gifts on December 19, the Ukrainian St. Nicholas Day, almost a week before many of their peers, who must wait until Christmas Eve to open their presents.

This vintage Father Christmas is almost monk-like, hinting at his roots as St. Nicholas.

CHAPTER 3

SANTA IN POP CULTURE

ON SCREENS BIG AND SMALL, IN SONG, LITERATURE, ADVERTISING AND ARTWORK, KRIS KRINGLE IS CERTAINLY IN DEMAND!

DEAR SANTA PLEASE PAUSE HERE. JIMMY.

THE BEST (AND WORST!)

CELLULOID SANTAS

FROM CHARMING AND CHERUBIC TO CAREER
CRIMINALS, NOT ALL CINEMA SANTAS FIND THEMSELVES
ON THE NICE LIST COME DECEMBER 25. HERE, OUR
RUNDOWN OF THE MOST UNFORGETTABLE PORTRAYALS
OF ST. NICHOLAS TO HIT THE BIG SCREEN.

Edmund Gwenn

Miracle on 34th Street, 1947

Gwenn's Santa enters the scene as a serendipitous last-minute fill-in for the Macy's Thanksgiving Day Parade—a nice old man with whiskers who needs no padding to fit in the red suit. But when, upon arriving at the iconic department store, he fills out his employment records with Kringle, Kris; next of kin: Dasher, et al., in the Christmas classic *Miracle on 34th Street*, he finds himself in a personal and eventual legal brawl to prove he is, in fact, the one and only Santa Claus. For an hour and 41 minutes, the viewer is brought into the life of Macy's parade director Doris Walker (Maureen O'Hara) and her daughter, Susan (Natalie Wood), as they begin to open their hearts and minds to the magic of Santa and the spirit of the season.

With his naturally warm benevolence and charming yet mischievous demeanor, Gwenn's portrayal became so iconic that not only did he win an Academy Award for his performance, but it also became the gold standard for generations of movie Santas to come. Tim Allen called him "top rung," William Shatner referred to him as "the essential Santa Claus," and Gwenn's *Miracle* costar O'Hara admitted that "Halfway through the shoot, we all believed Edmund really was Santa."

Tim Allen

The Santa Clause trilogy, 1994, 2002, 2006

How did the story of a divorced dad who burns the turkey then scares the real Santa off the roof on Christmas Eve manage to make its way to the No. 2 spot? "It's a comedy, but it keeps the character integral to the myth," Allen explained. "It seemed plausible to older kids, and adults could see it too. If you mixed up all the myths and metaphors of Santa all over the world...this is a melting-pot rendition of those."

In this movie, a Santa origins story of sorts ("You put on the suit, you're the big guy," David Krumholtz's Head Elf Bernard lays out for Scott Calvin on his first trip to the North Pole), Allen's Santa may reluctantly take the reins, but he turns out to be a more than capable Claus. Over the course of a year, viewers follow Scott's physical and emotional transformation from a bitter businessman into the kind, jolly old elf kids across the world wait up for on Christmas Eve.

THE NICE LIST

Tom Hanks *The Polar Express*, 2004

Disclaimer: No bonus points were given to Hanks for managing five different roles in the movie adaptation of this literary classic. Yet, in the actor's classic fashion, he brings new life into each part. Hanks, who played the dad, the conductor, the hobo, a young boy and, of course, St. Nick himself, had been a longtime fan of the children's book when he managed to snag the rights to the story.

The beauty of *The Polar Express*' Santa is in his effortless ability to bring belief back to the children who visit him and to stay true to the Christmas spirit—reminding Hero Boy (Daryl Sabara) to "just remember, the true spirit of Christmas lies in your heart."

Perhaps Hanks was a natural, in part due to his résumé: "When I was 21 years old, I had a job playing Santa Claus in a shopping center...I was let go after two weeks.... I haven't done it since, so [*The Polar Express*] might be the one chance I get," he said at the time of filming. Going on to portray one of the most noteworthy Nicks of all time? Now, that's a redemption story for the ages.

> "Seeing is believing, but sometimes the most real things in the world are the things we can't see."
>
> THE CONDUCTOR,
> *THE POLAR EXPRESS*

Paul Giamatti *Fred Claus*, 2007

It turns out, being the big man comes with a price. Giamatti's Nick "Santa" Claus is the St. Nicholas we can all relate to. He's weary, he's worked hard for centuries, and yet he still can't seem to please his wife (Miranda Richardson), mother (Kathy Bates) or ever-envious brother (Vince Vaughn)—oh, or his legion of elves or the millions of children around the world who rely on him. No pressure! "I just got such a kick out of seeing Santa Claus as a human being...his issues of being a saint and having to take care of everyone," said director David Dobkin.

Giamatti's magic, though, comes in his ability to make the audience not just feel for his Santa but also to rethink the role—one of the most beloved characters of all time—without disliking his demeanor or dismissing its importance.

> *"There's a poor orphan named Henry who lives down the road. I'm bringing all my gifts to him. He needs them more than I."*

YOUNG NICK, *FRED CLAUS*

Richard Attenborough
Miracle on 34th Street, 1994

The 1994 remake of the beloved classic stayed true to its original source material, with a little extra '90s corporate greed sprinkled in for good measure. While the movie itself opened to mixed reviews, it was Attenborough's portrayal of Kringle, likely the tallest shoes to fill, that was deemed its saving grace. Reviewer Caryn James, in *The New York Times,* declared, "As Kris Kringle, with half-glasses and a snowy beard, Richard Attenborough is miraculously convincing.... Mr. Attenborough plays him knowingly, as a kind man who just might be magical enough to grant Susan's (Mara Wilson) Christmas wish."

The character himself embodies all that is good about the Santa legend, and he breaks it down effortlessly in-scene: "I'm not just a whimsical figure who wears a charming suit and affects a jolly demeanor...I'm a symbol of the human ability to suppress the selfish and hateful tendencies that rule the major part of our lives," he says. The way this *Miracle* presents Santa as much more than a magic man in a suit is unparalleled—and remains ever-important to spreading the holiday spirit all year long.

THE
NICE
LIST

Kurt Russell
The Christmas Chronicles, 2018

As a blend of his iconic Wyatt Earp and Snake Plissken, Russell plays a Santa with really good hair in this 2018 Netflix movie. "I want to do the real guy," he said of the role. "He's 1,700 years old, the magic of that… and how they've commercialized him." Compounding Santa's existential issues are a couple of kids who cause his sleigh to crash, leading him to steal a car and land in jail—but it's all in an effort to save the Christmas spirit. The movie received lackluster reviews, but *The New York Times* said: "The star makes the unfolding shenanigans tolerable, playing Santa as a kind of jovial emcee with sincerity, pathos and gravitas." With his "mostly" real beard and modern sensibility, Russell's Santa just wants to get on with business. "He's up to date," Russell said. "He's like, 'No, I don't do Ho, ho, ho. Fake news.'"

David Huddleston *Santa Claus: The Movie*, 1985

Beginning in the 10th century, in the house of a medieval toymaker, *Santa Claus: The Movie* is the ultimate origin story. Huddleston builds a believable backstory for Father Christmas, whose story arc may grow but whose core personality never falters. "I wanted to portray him in both the early scenes and after he becomes Santa as a very warm but vulnerable person," Huddleston revealed.

Once the movie wrapped, the actor refused to do press in his suit, in order to maintain the magic of the character. "There is a special responsibility in playing [Santa Claus]," Huddleston shared. "I wanted this Santa to be as real as possible."

Ed Asner *Elf*, 2003

What better way to illustrate Santa's trademark benevolence than to show love and charity to a human baby boy who stows away in your bag one Christmas? Santa watched over Buddy the Elf (Will Ferrell) into his adulthood, constantly giving him motivation and encouragement despite his "different" status amongst his friends and family. And when Buddy discovers he's actually human—Santa delivers the truth about Buddy's real family with compassionate candor ("Your father...he's on the Naughty List") and still supports Buddy's decision to seek out his roots.

Asner called the story "a wonderful contribution, encouraging a return to the spirit of Christmas." That sentiment is exemplified when Buddy helps to save the day. It's Santa's moving speech ("Buddy, you're more of an elf than anyone I ever met and the only one who I would want working on my sleigh tonight") that gives him the confidence to reattach the sleigh's engine, giving Jovie the elf (Zooey Deschanel) just enough time to inspire "Christmas cheer by singing loud for all to hear."

SANTA BRINGS CHRISTMAS FUN TO MARS!

Blast off for Mars... with Santa and a pair of Earth Kids! Science-Fun-Fiction at its height!

JOSEPH E. LEVINE presents

SANTA Claus CONQUERS **THE MARTIANS**

IN SPACE-BLAZING **COLOR**

SAT.-SUN. MATINEE SPECIAL

SEE: The Martians Kidnap Santa!
Santa's North Pole Workshop!
The Fantastic Martian Toy Factory!
Earth Kids Meeting With Martian Kids!
Space ship Journey from Earth to Mars!

THE JURY'S STILL OUT

John Call
Santa Claus Conquers the Martians, 1964

Admittedly, good vs. bad is a little hard to nail down in this movie; it's more like...weird. In the campy cult flick, Santa is abducted by a group of aliens who have decided the only way to save the overly rigid children of Mars is to bring a Santa-like figure into their lives. As a result, Call's Santa isn't all naughty per se, sometimes he's quite profound. As *Fred Claus*'s Paul Giamatti called him, "A little bit of a Shakespearean Santa.... He's got a lot of gravitas." Unfortunately, he's also a hostage, doing what needs to be done to escape—and it's hard to ignore that, at times, it includes risking the lives of children and promoting violence.

In the end though, Mars finds its own Santa, and Call's Claus heads back down to Earth to presumedly fulfill his Christmas Day duties. A happy ending to what producer Paul L. Jacobson called a "Yuletide science-fiction fantasy."

Edward Ivory
The Nightmare Before Christmas, 1993

The holiday mashup to rival today's best Marvel superhero crossovers features Jack Skellington as a spurious Santa more than it does the man himself; yet Santa (or Sandy Claws, as Jack not-so-affectionately refers to him) remains a central character in Tim Burton's *The Nightmare Before Christmas*. Voiced by Ivory, he is kidnapped by a trio of Halloween Town troublemakers at the behest of Jack, in order to bring Christmas to his world. Santa has his stern and not-so-jolly moments in his quest to escape capture, but he clearly bears no hard feelings in the end, sending snow and Christmas wishes to Jack and the rest of Halloween Town as he soars away on his sleigh. A very benevolent reaction, worthy of a true Santa.

Hulk Hogan *Santa with Muscles, 1996*

Widely considered one of the worst movies ever made, *Santa with Muscles* lasted a mere two weeks in theaters, grossing just $220,198 during that time. In the film, professional wrestler–turned-actor Hogan stars as Blake Thorn, an arrogant millionaire who, after hitting his head while running from the police, comes to believe that he is Santa Claus. Sure, amnesia may have made him a better man—after all, he invites a group of orphans to live in his mansion after their orphanage is destroyed—but the plot did nothing to help the reception this movie received. "*Santa with Muscles* is a 98-pound weakling of a comedy, with other movies certain to kick sand in its face during its limited theatrical run," wrote *Variety* film critic Joe Leydon. "Call it the movie equivalent of coal in a Christmas stocking, and you won't be far off the mark." Talk about a smackdown!

AND
THE
NAUGHTY
LIST

Billy Bob Thornton

Bad Santa, 2003

Just when you thought no one could put a new spin on the red suit, along comes Thornton as the drunkest, most profane and irredeemable Santa Claus in movie history! As Willie T. Soke, Thornton's Santa is a sex-addicted alcoholic thief who works as a mall Santa, alongside his dwarf/elf accomplice (the brains of their operation), Marcus (Tony Cox), as they plot their heists. Thurman Merman (Brett Kelly)—the hapless kid whose house Willie illegally uses as a crash-pad—idolizes him, but Willie's Santa is totally incapable of grasping the spirit of Christmas. "It's the alternative to the real syrupy Christmas movies," Thornton said. But for Santa Claus purists, the movie was sacrilegious. Everything Thornton's Claus is, everything he represents, is the antithesis of the Head Elf himself. *The Washington Post* wrote that producer Miramax "has sold Santa down a moral sewer." Still, that didn't stop the film from becoming a cult hit and spawning a sequel.

Jeff Gillen *A Christmas Story*, 1983

As if his poorly placed faux beard weren't enough of an affront to the image of Santa, Gillen's grumpy Higbee's character caused bulging eyes and shocked faces everywhere when he unceremoniously denied a nervous Ralphie (Peter Billingsley) as he requested his dream gift—an official Red Ryder Carbine-Action 200-shot Range Model Air Rifle ("You'll shoot your eye out, kid"). Santa then heaved a "Ho, Ho, Ho" in Ralphie's heartbroken face and gave him the—literal—boot down a terrifyingly twisty slide. Gillen's on-screen time may have been short, but his cultural impact was great. For better or worse, he'll go down as one of the most memorable to play the role.

Artie Lange *Elf*, 2003

Leave it to Buddy the Elf (Will Ferrell) to call out this department store employee (Lange) who smells like "beef and cheese" for impersonating his good friend Santa. "You sit on a throne of lies," he tells the pseudo-St. Nick, before pulling off his beard to expose the truth. The two get into a knock-down-drag-out brawl, which had to be filmed in one take. It took the movie's art department two weeks to set up the elaborate Gimbels Santaland set, including an intricate LEGO city-scape, Lite-Brite and Etch A Sketch displays, and paper snowflakes, but Buddy and his nemesis destroy it all in mere minutes, to the horror of the kids!

PICTURE PERFECT

ILLUSTRATORS AND PAINTERS THROUGHOUT THE DECADES HAVE BEEN INSTRUMENTAL IN SHAPING THE BIG GUY'S IMAGE.

1881

circa 1330s

1810

The Charity of St. Nicholas of Bari,
Ambrogio Lorenzetti

St. Nicholas,
Alexander Anderson

Merry Old Santa Claus,
Thomas Nast

Over the years, Santa has evolved from a Turkish bishop to a tiny elf to the jolly old man of today. Sometimes subtle, sometimes stark, each new development in his style shift is inspired by artists who open their minds to the magic. One after the next, they shaped St. Nick, not just in looks but in story—drawing his reindeer, his sleigh, his toys. But the singular thread that ties the transformation together is the depiction of his unyielding generosity.

Artistic renderings of St. Nicholas date back as far as the 13th century: He's often seen giving gifts as the patron saint of children but otherwise he's unrecognizable as the man who would one day be Santa. Ambrogio Lorenzetti's rendering of the fourth-century bishop, *The Charity of St. Nicholas*

of Bari, painted around 1330, depicts the saint sneaking gold into the window of a poor family's house. It's on permanent display at Paris' Louvre museum, where daily, 15,000 tourists pass by (often unknowingly) the precursor to Père Noel.

Searching for St. Nicholas

The first known images of St. Nicholas in the United States can be attributed to Alexander Anderson, commissioned for New York City's first St. Nicholas feast. The artist didn't stray far from the religious figure of earlier days: Anderson's St. Nick has a beard slightly longer and whiter than before, and in some of his engravings, the saint is depicted giving gifts only to good children and stuffed stockings hang from a fireplace.

Thomas Nast, the cartoonist who gave the Republicans their elephant and the Democrats their donkey, also gave children everywhere their Santa Claus. With Nast we saw today's jelly-belly figure take shape. "Before Nast created his version,

circa 1890s

Gnome with Torch, Jenny Nyström

1925

Old Kris, N.C. Wyeth

St. Nicholas had been pictured as everything from a stern patriarch in bishop's robes to a gnomelike creature in a frock coat and pantaloons," Joel Coughlin, owner of the now defunct The Thomas Nast Home Page, told *The New York Times*.

Though he came to the U.S. at just 6 years old, Nast tapped into his early encounters with St. Nick in Germany to sketch a new Civil War–era Santa for the States (the Union, at the time). He took pieces from the saint of his youth and combined them with Clement C. Moore's description in "A Visit from St. Nicholas." The result? A portly man with a long white beard and a fur-trimmed coat at the reigns of a reindeer-drawn sleigh. Nast continued to illustrate Claus for decades, building out much of Kringle's signature style and story.

We can thank Nast for Santa's North Pole address, his Naughty and Nice lists, his bag of toys, and that signature scarlet suit.

Jenny Nyström, meanwhile, gave Santa a Swedish twist near the end of the 19th century by highlighting her country's traditional gnomes, or *jultomte*. Eventually she blended their characteristics into her images of St. Nick himself. But as Santa evolved, not all images stood the test of time. N.C. Wyeth's *Old Kris*, published in *Country Gentleman* in 1925, was closer, but his oversize nose didn't make the cut.

A Household Figure

If designing Santa were like decking the halls, Nast strung the proverbial lights, but J.C. Leyendecker and Norman Rockwell trimmed the tree. The duo

1925

1948

THE SATURDAY EVENING POST

DEC. 26, '25   5c. the Copy

CHRISTMAS

Hug from Santa,
J.C. Leyendecker

Santa and His Helpers,
Norman Rockwell

Norman Rockwell

brought Santa into the homes of Americans on the cover of *The Saturday Evening Post*. In 1908, the *Post*'s readership had skyrocketed, hitting a circulation of 1 million. Four years later, Santa was right there on the cover, drawn by Leyendecker. He refined the Santas of the past, and each subsequent cover seemed to be filled with more visual detail. His Santa was so jolly that when he smiled, his eyes nearly disappeared.

When Leyendecker left his post at the *Post*, Rockwell took over. His unique ability to capture small-town America was so loved by the public that his remain the images many envision when dreaming of St. Nick of yore. Today, many of Rockwell's original paintings reside at the Norman Rockwell Museum in Stockbridge, Massachusetts.

Share a Coke with Santa

The Coca-Cola company also helped to define the Santa Claus we know today. In 1931, the beverage company commissioned Haddon Sundblom to illustrate an image of Father Christmas for a reported $1,000—big money during the Great Depression. Sundblom leaned heavily on the illustrations of his predecessors, but he added a new live model to the mix: Lou Prentiss, a friend and retired salesman. After his first Coca-Cola Santa appeared in 1931 in *The Saturday Evening Post*, Sundblom created more than 40 original oil paintings featuring his larger-than-life depiction of the man in red (and he went on to create the Quaker Oats man). Many of his Santa paintings can be seen at the World of Coca-Cola in Atlanta.

1959

Refreshing Surprise,
Haddon Sundblom

SANTA CLAUS IN GIVERNY

Photographer Ed Wheeler has reimagined many classic paintings, putting jolly old St. Nick front and center, as in this Monet. Check out the rest of the series, called Santa Classics, at santaclassics.com.

THE BEST OF SANTA

ON THE SMALL SCREEN

FOR MORE THAN HALF A CENTURY, FAMILIES HAVE GATHERED AROUND THE TELEVISION DURING THE HOLIDAY SEASON TO WATCH THESE CLASSIC CHRISTMAS SPECIALS TOGETHER.

The Grinch despises all things Christmas and is determined to take the holiday away from the residents of Whoville.

How the Grinch Stole Christmas! | 1966

PLOT Up on a mountain, overlooking Whoville, lives a Grinch who hates Christmas. Sick of witnessing the outpouring of holiday cheer in the village below, the Grinch decides to steal the holiday. Yet despite their missing presents, decorations and food, the Whos wake up Christmas morning and celebrate anyway. Realizing you can't steal the Christmas spirit, the Grinch's heart grows big enough to hold happiness—he returns the stolen goods and celebrates Christmas with the Whos, who welcome him with open arms.

FUN FACT The movie was based on a book published by Dr. Seuss in 1957. At that time, the Grinch's coloring was black and white. Director and co-producer Chuck Jones decided to make the sinister character avocado green after he had rented a car in the same unsightly shade.

DID YOU KNOW Thurl Ravenscroft, who sang "You're a Mean One, Mr. Grinch," also voiced Tony the Tiger in Frosted Flakes commercials at the time.

SECOND LOOK As the Grinch passes the slice of roast beast that he carved, it changes color.

BEHIND THE SCENES It cost $300,000 to make *How the Grinch Stole Christmas!*—a budget that was unheard of at the time—and the equivalent of about $2.3 million today. To compare: 1965's *A Charlie Brown Christmas* cost a mere $96,000.

SCENE-STEALER Little Cindy Lou Who (at left), the towheaded tot who bravely confronts the Grinch as he siphons their Christmas gifts. Even after realizing his lies and thievery, Cindy Lou embodies the Christmas spirit of forgiveness and holds no ill will toward the previously miserable and misguided Grinch, sitting right next to him during the Christmas feast.

BEST LINE "He puzzled and puzzled till his puzzler was sore. Then the Grinch thought of something he hadn't before. Maybe Christmas, he thought... doesn't come from a store. Maybe Christmas, perhaps... means a little bit more!" —*Narrator*

PLOT When a fawn named Rudolph is born with a red blinking nose, he must come to terms with the fact that it's OK to be different. After running away from home, landing on an island of misfits, and fighting off an abominable snowman, Rudolph comes back to save the day by using his nose to guide Santa through a foggy Christmas Eve night.

FUN FACT After it was thought the puppets used in this stop-motion special had all been lost, Rudolph and Santa resurfaced in a family's attic, having survived decades as children's toys and casual holiday decorations. The duo were restored in 2006 and proceeded to make the rounds at conventions across the country.

DID YOU KNOW *Rudolph the Red-Nosed Reindeer* has been broadcast every year since its debut in 1964, making it the longest-running Christmas special on television.

SECOND LOOK When Rudolph helps guide Santa's sleigh through the sky, there are only six other reindeer helping. What happened to the other two?

BEHIND THE SCENES Though they look larger on television, during filming, the puppet used for Rudolph was only four inches tall and Santa was eight inches; Bumble was the tallest, measuring just over a foot, at 14 inches.

SCENE-STEALER(S) The Misfit Toys, the cast of nonconforming characters who embrace their oddities while lamenting the fun they'll be missing on Christmas Day stuck on the island named for them: *How'd you like to be a spotted elephant? / Or a choo-choo with square wheels on its caboose? / We're all Misfits!*

BEST LINE "How can you overlook that? His beak blinks like a blinkin' beacon!" —*Donner*

Rudolph the Red-Nosed Reindeer | 1964

The original version of *Rudolph* does not have Santa going back to save the Misfit Toys, as he promised. Viewers complained to NBC, so a scene was added that showed Misfit Island as Santa's first stop.

It's not just believing that brings Santa to town, it's Albert's smarts, learning how to fix the clock from his studies of Copernicus.

'Twas the Night Before Christmas | 1974

PLOT When Santa reads a Letter to the Editor calling him a "fraudulent myth" and signed by "All of Us" in Junctionville, New York, he refuses to visit the town on Christmas Eve and returns the townspeople's Christmas letters unopened. Clockmaker Joshua Trundle and a family of mice must find a way to save their Christmas. But Father Mouse's brainy son, Albert, continues to disrupt the plans— first, as the letter writer, then by unintentionally sabotaging the clock tower built to lure Santa back to town. In the end, Albert manages to fix the clock, and when Santa hears the chimes and carols, he shows up to deliver presents.

FUN FACT The fictional setting of Junctionville, New York, is believed to be a nod to the author of "A Visit from St. Nicholas," aka "'Twas the Night Before Christmas," whose hometown was also in the Empire State.

DID YOU KNOW The song, "Even a Miracle Needs a Hand," is parodied in Season 4 of *South Park*, in the "A Very Crappy Christmas" episode.

SECOND LOOK Though the opening credits say "told and sung by Joel Grey" (the voice of Joshua Trundle), most of the story is narrated by Father Mouse, voiced by George Gobel.

BEHIND THE SCENES It was a star-studded session in the recording studio for "Even a Miracle Needs a Hand." Broadway vets and Tony Award winners Joel Grey and Tammy Grimes voice Joshua Trundle and Albert the Mouse, respectively, in this duet.

SCENE-STEALER With just moments to go until Christmas, Albert manages to fix the clock tower, triggering the first notes of the Christmas carol and beckoning Santa to stop in town.

BEST LINE "You don't know as much as you think because you only think with your head, so you have a lot of trouble believing in things you can't see or touch." —*Father Mouse to Albert*

PLOT After their snowman comes to life on Christmas Eve, a group of schoolchildren must keep their new friend from melting—and from an inept and dishonest magician who wants his hat (the one that holds the magic that brought Frosty to life) back.

FUN FACT Frosty's hometown is Armonk, New York. Lyricist Steve Nelson lived there for many years and was imagining it when he wrote the song, according to reports. To this day, the town hosts an annual Frosty Day parade to celebrate.

DID YOU KNOW Frosty came to life in song, long before he appeared as our favorite small-screen snowman. When they wrote it in 1950, songwriters Walter "Jack" Rollins and Nelson were looking to capitalize on the success of the previous year's hit, "Rudolph the Red-Nosed Reindeer."

SECOND LOOK Frosty has four fingers, except during the scene when he tries to count to 10. When he is finished counting, the fifth digit disappears.

BEHIND THE SCENES The directors wanted the holiday special to have a greeting-card look. So they hired Paul Coker Jr., a greeting-card and magazine artist, as a character and background designer.

SCENE-STEALER Professor Hinkle. Everything about that greedy magician—from his diabolical disregard for Frosty's life to the stomach-turning ways he talks in threes—is *evil, evil, evil.* He's the epitome of a villain you love to hate.

BEST LINE "Oh, don't cry, Karen. Frosty's not gone for good. You see, he was made out of Christmas snow, and Christmas snow can never disappear completely." — *Santa Claus*

Frosty the Snowman | 1969

Frosty is the first Rankin/Bass Productions holiday special to be animated, as opposed to stop-motion animation (like on *Rudolph*), which utilizes puppets.

Kris Kringle tells Tanta Kringle and the rest of the family that he wishes to restore them as "The First Toymakers to the King."

Santa Claus Is Comin' to Town | 1970

PLOT Where does Santa Claus come from? The answer can be found in this origin story about an abandoned baby named Claus taken in by a family of toymakers. He's so adamant to bring happiness to children everywhere, he risks his life and freedom to deliver presents to a town that has outlawed toys.

FUN FACT When one of the kids unintentionally called Blitzen "Blitser," producers decided to leave it in, agreeing it added credence to the dialogue, since young children often mispronounce words.

DID YOU KNOW From its debut through the early 1980s, the Clauses' penguin friend was called Waddles. For reasons unknown, his name was subsequently changed to Topper.

SECOND LOOK The father of the children who receive toys in their stockings, the doctor who

treats Meisterburger Burgermeister, and the drawing of the king in Tanta Kringle's book are all the same wood-and-plastic puppet.

BEHIND THE SCENES Composer Maury Lewis has said that *Santa Claus Is Comin' to Town* was his favorite Christmas special to work on. Considering he also worked on *Rudolph the Red-Nosed Reindeer* and *Frosty the Snowman*, that's saying a lot!

SCENE-STEALER Antagonist Winter Warlock. The furry white giant captures young Claus, positioning himself as an emerging villain. But when Santa offers him a toy train, showing him kindness for the first time, the ice melts from the Warlock's heart and the two become fast friends.

BEST LINE "Changing from bad to good's as easy as taking your first step." —*Kris Kringle*

PLOT When Santa's doctor convinces him that he's no longer relevant, the Big Guy decides to take the year off. Mrs. Claus, Vixen and the elves set out to prove him wrong by finding kids and adults alike who still believe.

FUN FACT The painting that hangs on Santa's wall is the same painting used at the end of *Santa Claus Is Comin' to Town.*

DID YOU KNOW Elves Jingle Bells and Jangle Bells resemble the Heat Miser and the Snow Miser.

SECOND LOOK When Mrs. Claus talks about the kids from around the world who are making gifts for Santa, a child dressed as a cowboy is shown when she says "from the East," and a child in Oriental garb is shown when she says "West." Looks like someone needs to brush up on their geography.

BEHIND THE SCENES Animators added a character who resembles Charlie Chaplin's Little Tramp

character. He can be spotted during the mayor's song "It's Gonna Snow Right Here in Dixie."

SCENE-STEALER(S) The Heat Miser and Snow Miser—and their catchy contrasting choruses—were such popular secondary characters that in 2008, they received their own spin-off special, *A Miser Brothers' Christmas.*

BEST LINE "I believe in Santa Claus like I believe in love." —*Santa Claus*

When an under-the-weather Santa is convinced no one cares about Christmas, the holiday is nearly canceled.

The Year Without a Santa Claus | 1974

In 2000, Chandler (Matthew Perry) lent a hand to Ross (David Schwimmer), who was the Holiday Armadillo on *Friends*.

How the Flintstones Saved Christmas first aired on December 25, 1964.

"I'm all about da winter holidays," Bugs Bunny revealed in 2006's *Bah, Humduck! A Looney Tunes Christmas*.

EVERYONE WANTS TO BE HIM

IF IMITATION IS THE SINCEREST FORM OF FLATTERY, SANTA CLAUS MUST BE THE MOST ADULATED OF ALL!

Snoopy got the Santa treatment in 2003's *I Want a Dog for Christmas, Charlie Brown*.

Yogi Bear decided hibernation could wait in 1980's *Yogi's First Christmas*.

Michael (Steve Carell) couldn't believe that Phyllis (Phyllis Smith) stole his Christmas thunder on a 2009 episode of *The Office*.

Mickey Rooney played a grumpy store owner who found the Christmas spirit on *Full House* in 1994.

"On Jumper, on, uh, Blunder, on, uh, Bouncer, on Thunder..."
FRED FLINTSTONE

The I Love Lucy Christmas Special (1956) marked the first time a sitcom used flashbacks.

Alvin's plan to play Santa went awry in 1981's *A Chipmunk Christmas*.

Homer attended Santa School on the very first episode of *The Simpsons* in 1989.

James Spader donned the suit in 2004 on *Boston Legal.*

Herman (Sam McMurray) frightened carolers in 1996's *The Munsters' Scary Little Christmas.*

SNL's Kenan Thompson fielded tough questions from kids in 2017, like "Is President Trump on the Naughty List?"

Mickey Mouse has dressed up as the "jolly old elf" many times, dating back to 1931's *Mickey's Orphans.*

HOW SANTA WENT FROM LEGEND TO

LEGENDARY PITCHMAN

EVERYBODY LOVES HIM AND HIS ONLY VICE IS COOKIES—SO IT'S NO WONDER SANTA CLAUS HAS APPEARED IN HUNDREDS OF ADS FOR EVERYTHING FROM CANDY TO CIGARETTES (HE PROBABLY REGRETS THOSE) TO PLAY-DOH AND IPHONES OVER THE PAST 150 YEARS.

The soda giant uses Christmas imagery in ads as well as promotional items.

Coca-Cola

REFRESHING SURPRISE

127

13

By the 1860s, Santa's image had become instantly recognizable. It was about this same time that advances in printing technology meant there were more newspapers and magazines than ever; meanwhile, modern advertising began to take off, spurred by the rapidly growing consumer class. This gave manufacturers more opportunities to advertise and thus expand from regional companies into national brands. But before the age of movies, radio or TV, there were no widely known professional athletes or actors to promote products, so advertisers latched onto the perfect pitchman: Santa Claus. "There are very few images that immediately communicate the Christmas season, and arguably none are as immediate and iconic as Santa Claus," explains Jim Radosevic, former president of Young & Rubicam New York, and currently managing

Coke® 12 FL OZ (355 mL) 140 CALORIES PER CAN

Santa Claus now includes the unsurpassed mineral water White Rock among his tokens of the Yuletide.

This 1937 ad proved that Santa brings gifts to adults, too!

Santa Claus always keeps up with the times, even appearing on this wrapper for a sugar-free candy.

Haddon Sundblom's renderings of Santa Claus for The Coca-Cola Company were a huge success.

Now... it's my time

"Coca–Cola didn't invent Santa Claus, but we did... help shape how people around the world see him."

JUSTINE FLETCHER, DIRECTOR OF HERITAGE COMMUNICATIONS AT THE COCA-COLA COMPANY

COLGATE'S
For Christmas
Useful Gifts, not Gimcracks

DEAR SANTA:-
DON'T FORGET HOLSUM BREAD

Merry Christmas, World.

A most original fragrance

The gorgeous, sexy-young fragrance. By Revlon
Perfume, Perfumed Dusting Powder, Body Silk, Concentrated Cologne and Cologne.
(All Charlie sprays, environmentally safe.)

Shelley Hack was the face of Revlon's Charlie perfume for nearly a decade. In 1978, she got some help from Santa.

"The fun is when advertisers stay true to the traditional (Santa) but put him in 'fish out of water' situations."

JIM RADOSEVIC, FORMER PRESIDENT,
YOUNG & RUBICAM NEW YORK

partner at brand incubator Igniter Brand Works. "Incredibly, his character has remained virtually unchanged over the decades—which may be why he can trigger a wave of nostalgia in people, regardless of their age."

Taking Advantage of Santa's Good Nature

At first, Santa appeared only in ads that dovetailed perfectly with his jovial, generous image. One of the earliest was for U.S. Confection Company's Sugar Plums, a candy popular around Christmas; pairing the two was a no-brainer. Ivory Soap billed itself as "99 and $^{44}/_{100}$ percent pure," so when the company used Santa in an 1885 ad that showed him putting Ivory soap in children's stockings, the brand was associating itself with Santa's wholesome nature (though 19th-century children were probably no more thrilled at getting soap for Christmas than today's kids would be).

Another company that capitalized on Santa's image was General Mills, which first tapped Santa to promote Gold Medal Flour in 1914; it later used him in Cheerios (then known as Cheerioats) ads, starting in 1941. In 1971, the company teamed him with another weight-challenged character, the Pillsbury Dough Boy, in another much-loved campaign.

Santa's Most Famous Role

The ad campaign that cemented Santa's image as a legendary pitchman was the decades-long one he starred in for Coca-Cola starting in the 1920s. "When it comes to using Santa Claus in advertising, Coke wins hands down," says Radosevic. Coca-Cola was not the first soft-drink company to use Santa in an ad—that honor goes to White Rock, which featured him in a 1915 advert—or the last (Santa has also done Pepsi ads), but it was Coca-Cola that used him to best effect.

For one thing, Santa helped Coca-Cola solve a seemingly intractable problem:

Sales dropped off in the winter months, when people were less likely to crave a cold drink. Enter Santa, whose global one-night trek in the middle of winter left him in dire need of a thirst-quenching beverage. Taglines like "travel refreshed" and "the pause that refreshes" reinforced the message.

The campaign became iconic when, in 1931, the company's ad agency, D'Arcy Advertising, hired Haddon Sundblom to illustrate the Christmas ads. Sundblom's plump, cheerful man dressed in red and white—which, coincidentally, are Coke's signature colors—was an instant and long-lasting success. In 1931, the Depression was in full swing, and the national mood was bleak. But Coke was an inexpensive treat (a bottle cost only a nickel then) that almost everyone could afford.

Over the years, Sundblom embellished the Santa legend, adding a Mrs. Claus (based on his own wife) and an elflike helper named Sprite Boy, who went on to have another soft drink—Sprite—named after him. Sundblom's ads ran for 33 years, and Coca-Cola continued using his images after his retirement in 1964. Because the ads were everywhere—in magazines, newspapers, on billboards and later on television, Coke is forever associated with Santa.

NO. 162

131

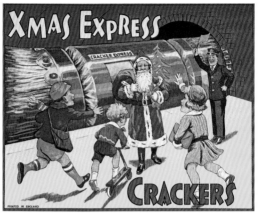

A Key Demographic

Besides Coke, many other Santa advertisements have targeted kids, from candy (Baby Ruth, Whitman's Samplers, M&M's) to gum (P.K., Dubble Bubble) to desserts (Jell-O, Oreos). Toy stores such as FAO Schwarz and Toys "R" Us, and Woolworth's stores, featured him in seasonal ads, while he also starred in ads for toy manufacturers, including Flexible Flyer sleds, Lionel trains, Matchbox cars, Play-Doh and Schwinn bikes.

Against the Image

But Santa sometimes veered into R-rated territory. Advertisers realized he could give an aura of respectability to some less-than-pure products,

This 1955 ad evokes all the heartwarming feelings of the holidays.

...And there on the table, awaiting his call Was a huge bowl of Jell-O, a fine treat for all!

Merry Christmas to all from Jell-O

JELL-O
BRAND
GELATIN DESSERT
SEVEN DELICIOUS FLAVORS

namely cigarettes and booze. According to a 1919 ad, Murad's Turkish Cigarettes are what all the "grown-ups" were smoking for Christmas. Santa didn't give up appearing in cigarette ads until well into the 1970s, starring over the years in campaigns for Camel, Chesterfield and Marlboro; in a 1950 ad for Pall Mall, he even touted the cigarettes' purported health benefits, claiming they "guarded against throat scratch." (The Surgeon General would disagree.)

Liquor companies also love Santa. In a 1937 ad, Martini Vermouth posed the question, "What is Christmas without Santa Claus, and what is Santa Claus without Vermouth?" (Well, for one thing, you could argue that a sober Santa would be more

likely to deliver the presents to the right kids!) Over the years, he has also appeared in ads for Dewar's, Vat 69 whisky, and Schlitz, Michelob and Budweiser beers.

Time Warp

In some ads, Santa reflects the era more than his intrinsic values of generosity and kindness; this is especially true in ads targeting women in the 1950s and 1960s. Hoover ran a long campaign featuring women whose apparent greatest wish was to receive a vacuum for Christmas. "Christmas morning, she'll be happier with a Hoover," the copy promises. (Don't bet on it.) Others show women hoping to find an ironing board under the tree. (Um, didn't you get my letter?) An ad that would be unimaginable in the #MeToo era shows Santa peeking up the skirt of a woman hanging ornaments on a tree.

Santa Gets His Tech On

Thankfully, Santa has changed with the times, embracing ever-evolving technology and proving that even an old guy like St. Nick can (1) figure out how to use the modern gadgets and (2) use them to enhance his life. When Kodak introduced its then-revolutionary Pocket Instamatic Camera in 1972, Santa showed how easy it was to use.

Fast-forward to the digital age, and you'll find Santa using an I.B.M. Aptiva computer in 1995 to "find: all children/good"; hawking Hewlett-Packard's Idea Kit software program, in 1997; and once smartphones made their appearance, he was an early adapter, showing the world how Siri could make an around-the-world-in-one-night trek so much easier in a 2011 iPhone commercial.

Despite a misstep here and there, Santa's legacy is remarkably intact; a century and a half later, he's still as charming and beloved as ever. Every year, he manages to entice us with a new slew of Christmas commercials. "I think of him as timeless, not old-fashioned," says Radosevic.

No doubt Santa will be keeping Christmas merry and bright for many years to come.

The very first song to mention Santa Claus is 1864's "Up on the Housetop." Songwriter Benjamin Hanby was inspired by the poem, "A Visit from St. Nicholas."

SING A SONG OF SANTA

CHRISTMAS MUSIC
HAS PROVEN TO BE AN
IMPORTANT PART OF
THE HOLIDAY SEASON.

13

Bruce Springsteen's live version of "Santa Claus Is Comin' to Town" was recorded on New York's Long Island on December 12, 1975.

Taylor Swift released a holiday album in 2007.

Before the taste of Thanksgiving turkey has faded from our taste buds, the bearded big man appears, seemingly everywhere at once—on television, in advertisements, in movies, on the Internet...but it's popular music that may just be Santa's most prolific playground. What is it about Christmas tunes that make us feel so good? And why is it that no matter how many times we hear the same songs over and over and over again, we never get sick of them?

In many cases, holiday music evokes fond memories and emotional responses. "You learn it as a child, and it's one of the few bodies of songs that people have deep inside their memories," Phil Gentry, a musicologist based at the University of Delaware, told NBC News. Music has the power to transport us back in time. "Many of us associate this music with childhood and a happy time of presents and traditions and all the specialness that happens around that time of year," added Rhonda Freeman, a clinical neuropsychologist. "When the brain makes these associations with something very positive and pleasurable, the rewards system is being activated [which triggers] a number of chemicals, including dopamine."

We guess that's why 500-plus radio stations across the nation flip their formats to nonstop holiday music right after Thanksgiving. "You can be bombarded with them every Christmas, and yet, somehow, you always welcome them," shared Phil Ford, an associate professor of musicology at the Indiana University Jacobs School of Music.

The crooner's first holiday album, *A Jolly Christmas from Frank Sinatra*, was released in 1957.

Dubbed "The Voice of Christmas," Bing Crosby was the first popular singer to record holiday tunes.

Pandora figures provide the proof. "Every year, we see a tremendous spike in holiday music listening," said Ron Nenni, music curator at Pandora. And of course, some of the most popular holiday tunes are about the jolly man in red.

"Santa Claus Is Comin' to Town," the most played holiday song of the last 50 years, according to the American Society of Composers, Authors and Publishers (ASCAP), has been recorded by Perry Como, Fred Astaire, Gene Autry, Bing Crosby, Frank Sinatra, The Four Seasons, The Jackson 5, Michael Bublé, Justin Bieber...the list goes on and on. But perhaps the most memorable recording is by Bruce Springsteen, who delivered a live, rock 'n' roll version in 1975. According to a poll conducted by *Entertainment Weekly*, Springsteen's cover of the tune is fans' favorite, garnering 47.67 percent of votes.

The list of songs about Santa is almost as endless as a greedy kid's Christmas list. Just like "Santa Claus Is Comin' to Town," many others have received treatments from a wide variety of recording artists. Barely less iconic is "Here Comes Santa Claus," a hit written and recorded by Gene Autry in 1947. The singing cowboy was inspired to write the ditty after riding his horse in the 1946 Santa Claus Lane Parade (now known as the Hollywood Christmas Parade) and hearing the crowds yell, "Here Comes Santa." A decade later, the tune was recorded most authoritatively by the king himself, Elvis Presley. Dwight Yoakam recorded a country-inflected cover in 1997, and Bob Dylan even threw a folk-rock version into the mix in 2009.

"I Saw Mommy Kissing Santa Claus," written by Tommie Connor and recorded by 13-year-old Jimmy Boyd in 1952, offered a humorous take and reached No. 1 on the *Billboard* pop singles chart. The Catholic Church, however, wasn't in on the joke. It condemned the song because it mixed kissing (and the thought of a married woman having an affair) with Christmas. Several radio markets refused to play it. The ban was eventually lifted when Columbia Records appealed to church leaders and had the child actor meet with them to

Elvis' Christmas Album spent four weeks at the top of the *Billboard* charts in 1957.

Best-Selling Singles

OF COURSE, NOT EVERY GREAT CHRISTMAS TUNE IS ABOUT SANTA. HERE ARE THE BEST-SELLING CHRISTMAS SINGLES IN THE UNITED STATES ACCORDING TO NIELSEN SOUNDSCAN.

1

All I Want for Christmas Is You
MARIAH CAREY

2

Do You Want to Build a Snowman?
(from the Frozen soundtrack)
KRISTEN BELL, AGATHA LEE MONN AND KATIE LOPEZ

3

Christmas Eve/Sarajevo 12/24
TRANS-SIBERIAN ORCHESTRA

4

Mistletoe
JUSTIN BIEBER

talk about the lyrics—lyrics that make it clear that Santa is the boy's father, and therefore, the song is not about adultery. The ditty was later covered by the Ronettes, Andy Williams, The Jackson 5, and a parade of others. The best rendition of the song? John Mellencamp's, at least according to the blog *Deadspin*.

The novelty tune "Santa Baby," written by Joan Javits and Philip Springer, was sung with signature sensuality by Eartha Kitt in 1953. The song suggests a new image of Santa, as a kind of sugar daddy. "Slip a sable under the tree for me," Kitt purrs, "a '54 convertible too, light blue..." (Someone forgot to tell her that it's the thought that counts!) The singer revealed it was one of her favorite songs to record, and it went on to become the biggest hit of her career. Madonna recorded a version in 1987 for the charity album *A Very Special Christmas*, shining a spotlight on the song once again. It has since been recorded by Taylor Swift, Kylie Minogue, Ariana Grande and Gwen Stefani, among others. In 2011, Michael Bublé recorded his own version changing the lyrics to "Santa buddy" calling him "dude" instead of "dear" to mixed reviews.

Andy Williams recorded a staggering eight Christmas albums during his career, earning him the title "Mr. Christmas."

Gwen Stefani released *You Make It Feel Like Christmas* in December 2017.

5

Rockin' Around the Christmas Tree
BRENDA LEE

6

Where Are You Christmas?
(from the How the Grinch Stole Christmas soundtrack)
FAITH HILL

7

Christmas Canon
TRANS-SIBERIAN ORCHESTRA

8

Feliz Navidad
JOSÉ FELICIANO

9

Jingle Bell Rock
BOBBY HELMS

10

Last Christmas
WHAM!

THE CHRONICLES OF
KRiS

FOR CENTURIES,
CREATIVE TELLINGS OF
FATHER CHRISTMAS
HAVE LEAPT OFF THE
PAGE AND INTO
OUR HEARTS.

Diving into a
Christmas tale is a
great way to get in the
holiday spirit.

KRINGLE

Ask any child who can talk, and they'll probably be able to describe the legend of Santa Claus: His red suit, reindeer, workshop and annual flight around the world. Yet this wasn't always Santa's story. For millennia, the figure of Father Christmas was that of a gaunt, benevolent old-timer in bishop's clothing. The man we know today has been largely shaped by centuries of American literature: Mrs. Claus arrived in James Rees' 1849 short story, "A Christmas Legend." According to some, Louisa May Alcott introduced his elves in 1856. And while Santa had "eight tiny reindeer" in Clement C. Moore's "A Visit from St. Nicholas" poem, it was more than a century later that a ninth joined the herd when Robert L. May released his 1939 booklet *Rudolph the Red-Nosed Reindeer*. A Christmas rarely goes by without a new Claus composition added to the canon. His unyielding allure makes him the ideal character for children and adults alike who yearn to connect with, and believe in, the magic of Santa.

Arrival in America

Washington Irving, in his 1809 *A Knickerbocker's History of New York*, offered the fledgling United States its first glimpse at the man they'd soon call Santa. In the book, published on St. Nicholas Day, Irving described the saint as smoking a pipe and "laying his finger beside his nose," before mounting his wagon and disappearing over the treetops. These now familiar traits took hold in a land largely devoid of Father Christmas—or any Christmas traditions at all—and with that, Santa Claus was born in America.

Fourteen years later, Moore would further establish this Americanized Santa when he scribed

his poem, which was first published anonymously for a Troy, New York, newspaper, and later called "arguably the best-known verses ever written by an American." Moore, a friend of Irving, first scribbled the famous stanzas of "A Visit from St. Nicholas" one snowy Christmas Eve after heading to town by sleigh to pick up a Christmas turkey. After an encounter with his caretaker, a bearded, cheerful, pipe-smoking man named Jan Duychinck, Moore began to re-envision the St. Nicholas figure as a jolly, rotund character delivering joy to children on Christmas Eve. The poem, with all its descriptors—twinkling eyes, dimples, rosy cheeks—gave us the prototype for the Santa we know today.

Yes, Children, There Is a Santa Claus

Each year, millions of children complete the most important of tasks: writing a letter to Santa. And whether the recipient happens to be a literary legend or an editor at a major metropolitan newspaper, the gravity of a Santa missive requires a response. No one, we see in this set of letters, is too old or too good, to be an ambassador for Santa Claus.

Mark Twain's "A Letter from Santa Claus" comes in the form of an essay to his 3-year-old daughter, Susie, assuring her that he will do his best to bring her everything on her Christmas list; asking her questions and sprinkling magic into every line.

Letters from Father Christmas offers a collection of handwritten letters from fantasy author J.R.R. Tolkien, written and illustrated for his children between 1920 and 1942. The stories are told from the point of view of Father Christmas and his elvish secretary and recall the adventures of Santa and his friends the North Polar Bear and cubs Paksu and Valkotukka. In *The New York Times Book Review*, Nancy Willard wrote that within the letters, "Father Christmas lives. And never more merrily..."

When 8-year-old Virginia O'Hanlon sent a letter to the editor of *The Sun* (in New York City) requesting a fact check on Santa Claus, veteran newsman Francis Pharcellus penned a response so well-received that it continues to run in newspapers across the world each season ("Yes Virginia, there is a Santa Claus"). In an interview 40 years later, O'Hanlon recalled finding the response "overwhelmingly convincing"—as, no doubt, have the hosts of children who have turned to the letter, seeking Santa reassurance, each year since.

The Fantastical Father Christmas

From his earliest disciplinarian days, in Ogden Nash's "The Boy Who Laughed at Santa Claus"—chronicling the life of a child so naughty, St. Nick turns him into the first jack-in-the-box—to today's Kringle, the man in red has always shown at least a modicum of magic. Most of the time this enchantment is contained to the inhabitants of the North Pole. It's rare we read a Santa tale that places him in a world of fantasy—but in L. Frank Baum's Santa origin novel, *The Life and Adventures of Santa Claus*, St. Nick is placed in Baum's established world of Oz—a land filled with wondrous folklore. From his birth in an enchanted forest and adoption by a wood nymph to his first trip around the world, Baum chronicles Santa's entire life. While the story doesn't leave any long-term marks on the legend, it provides a fun alternative, offering backstories for traditions like the Christmas Tree, reindeer and the invention of toys.

Marketing Mr. Claus

Most classic Christmas tales sneak into our collective cultural psyche over decades. Some, however, were written with a marketing team in place. The first of its kind was Rudolph's. Before the television special, before the catchy song, Rudolph appeared in a 1939 booklet written by Robert L. May, a copywriter for the Montgomery Ward department store.

It was the height of the Great Depression and, in a bid to save money, one manager decided to create their own children's book for the annual holiday promotion. It was a success—the store distributed more than 2 million copies in store locations all over the country. Since then, Rudolph has starred on numerous TV specials and can be found on everything from bedsheets to postal stamps.

Nearly six decades later, a new Christmas custom was born, with the arrival of the book and toy duo *The Elf on the Shelf: A Christmas Tradition*. *The Atlantic* criticized the manufactured tradition: "Unlike holiday favorites that cost little or no money—[like] reciting ''Twas the Night Before Christmas'...the Elf is an endless opportunity to purchase things." The author is right, of course, in that the marketing value of the Elf on the Shelf franchise is tremendous, with a growing fleet of DVDs, outfits and accessories. Still, the public embraced Santa's spy and welcomed him into their homes. As of 2019, *The Elf on the Shelf* book had sold 13 million copies; an Elf balloon has even flown in the Macy's Thanksgiving Day Parade. Creator Chandra Bell says: "Any good tradition should feel timeless. For me, it's a classic story that's evergreen." And if the Elf on a Shelf helps kids believe—and maybe even behave—it has earned its rightful spot in the Christmas canon.

New Tales for Today's Tots

Each year, a new crop of Santa stories are published, ready to be plucked by eager parents instilling the Christmas spirit in their children. Some, like Chris Van Allsburg's *The Polar Express* or Vivian Walsh's *Olive, the Other Reindeer*, become modern classics, traditions in their own right; others bring glee for a single December, often featuring the children's character du jour (*Elmo's Countdown to Christmas*, *Pete the Cat Saves Christmas*), and then simply fade away into the recesses of Christmases past.

No matter the story's lasting resonance, each tale is valuable in that it instills some wonder, generosity, spirit and kindness into a child. And after all, that *is* what the Big Guy is all about.

"In Baltimore there lived a boy, he wasn't anybody's joy," begins Odgen Nash's humorous Christmas poem.

Tales of Santa's journey have been thrilling children for ages.

the **ELF** on the **SHELF**
A Christmas Tradition
By Carol V. Aebersold and Chanda A. Bell illustrated by Coë Steinwart
Adopt a new family tradition this holiday season!

THE POLAR EXPRESS

J.R.R. TOLKIEN
LETTERS FROM Father Christmas
edited by J.R.R.Tolkien

"A Visit from St. Nicholas" is more commonly known as "'Twas the Night Before Christmas."

Clement C. Moore wrote "A Visit from St. Nicholas" to entertain his children.

How to Catch an Elf
From the New York Times Bestselling Team
Adam Wallace & Andy Elkerton

OLIVE, the other REINDEER.

THE LIFE and ADVENTURES of Santa Claus
L. FRANK BAUM

RUDOLPH the RED-NOSED REINDEER
WRITTEN FOR MONTGOMERY WARD
ROBERT L. MAY

Virginia O'Hanlon wrote a letter to *The Sun* when she was 8 years old. The response has become Christmas folklore.

CHAPTER 4

CLAUS & COMPANY

A CLOSER LOOK AT FATHER
CHRISTMAS—WHERE HE
LIVES, THE TOYS HE MAKES,
AND WHAT IT TAKES TO
BE HIS HELPER.

TOYS FOR GIRLS & BOYS

THESE ARE THE GIFTS
CHILDREN EVERYWHERE
HOPED TO FIND UNDER
THEIR CHRISTMAS TREES
OVER THE PAST
12 DECADES.

"One of the most glorious messes in the world is the mess created in the living room on Christmas Day," *60 Minutes* commentator Andy Rooney once said.

hildren around the world have been sending their wish lists to Santa Claus since the U.S. Postal Service began hand-delivering mail, back in the 1860s. Over the decades, those requests have changed drastically, from minimalist to materialistic and from simple to high-tech.

1900s

CRAYOLA CRAYONS

The first crayons ever made were invented by cousins Edwin Binney and C. Harold Smith. Hitting the stores in 1903, a box of eight crayons (black, brown, blue, red, purple, orange, green and yellow) sold for a nickel. Binney's wife came up with the company name, Crayola, by combining the French words for "chalk" (*craie*) and "oily" (*olegineux*).

DIE-CAST MODEL T FORD

One of the earliest Christmas toys is a miniature version of the first car to be manufactured for everyday people. In 1908, the first production of the Model T Ford, also known as the Tin Lizzy, was produced in Detroit. Tiny toy models soon followed.

ROCKING HORSE

The earliest rocking horse reportedly belonged to England's King Charles I around 1610. In the early 1900s, the wooden toy became popular in the United States and was waiting for many a child on Christmas morn.

SPINNING TOP

One of the oldest known toys (they've been found at archaeological sites), the top is simple in concept but provides hours of fun. The low price made it an ideal present for many in the time of war—and poverty.

8 CLASSIC CRAYON COLOURS

Classic 8 Colours

CELEBRATING TEACHERS SINCE 1903 · HOMMAGE AUX ÉDUCATEURS DEPUIS

TRADE CRAYOLA MARK

№ 8

1910s

The first teddy bear was named after President Roosevelt.

RAGGEDY ANN

The rag doll with a triangle nose and red yarn for hair is a book character that was created by Johnny Gruelle. The newspaper cartoonist came up with the idea in 1915 when his daughter, Marcella, brought him an old, worn out rag doll. He brought new life to the tattered toy by drawing a face on it and giving it a name—Raggedy Ann. Three years later, books and dolls about the character were sold.

TEDDY BEAR

After news that President Teddy Roosevelt refused to shoot a bear during a hunting trip spread throughout the country, New York couple Morris and Rose Michtom turned a piece of plush velvet into the shape of a bear. Calling it "Teddy's bear," they displayed it in the window of their Brooklyn penny shop. When passersby showed interest in buying the bear, the Michtoms asked the president for permission, sending the original bear to the White House for his children. Roosevelt agreed, and the couple made a fortune!

ERECTOR SET

A.C. Gilbert, the inventor of the Erector set, was touted as "The Man Who Saved Christmas." In 1918, the United States considered cancelling Christmas so that parents would invest in war bonds rather than buying toys. Gilbert argued that America should be the home of educational toys that would prepare boys for adulthood. The Council of National Defense agreed.

LIONEL TRAINS

Joshua Lionel Cowen designed his first train in the early 1900s as a toy store's window display—not as a toy. But when customers inquired about buying the display, he knew he was in business. Between 1910 and 1919 sales increased 15-fold. As one of the company's early advertisements read: "Everybody is happy when it's a Lionel Train Christmas."

1920s

JOY BUZZER

Invented in 1928 by the same prankster who gave us the snake in the nut can and the exploding cigar (Soren Sorensen Adams), the joy buzzer doesn't actually shock the intended target. Instead, when a button on the disc is pressed by shaking hands, a spring unwinds, creating a vibration that feels like a shock. All in good fun!

RADIO FLYER WAGON

Italian immigrant Antonio Pasin was a craftsman who made phonograph cabinets. He built a wooden wagon to carry his tools and soon, he was selling more wagons than cabinets. In 1927, when demand increased, he began making metal wagons, which could be mass-produced. They sold for under $3 at the time.

TINKERTOYS

The toy construction set made up of sticks and wooden spools was created in 1914 by Charles Pajeau and Robert Pettit. Pajeau was inspired by watching children play with pencils and spools of thread. The tubular packaging was designed to reduce shipping costs and early versions even came with a shipping label.

YO-YO

Although the yo-yo dates back as far as 500 BC, it was Pedro Flores, a Filipino immigrant working as a bellhop, who brought the wooden discs on a string to America in the 1920s. He would play with the toy on his lunch breaks and hotel guests were intrigued. Flores opened a small factory and began manufacturing yo-yos. They became so popular, he was bought out by businessman Donald Duncan who went on to sell millions of yo-yos by staging contests where "champions" would "walk the dog," "rock the cradle," and perform other tricks with the toy.

1930s

ARMY MEN

The plastic soldiers were first manufactured by Bergen Toy & Novelty Co. in 1938. The diminutive toys (just 2 to 4 inches tall) were often sold in bulk—in buckets, boxes or barrels. *Time* magazine included Army Men among the 100 greatest toys of all time.

MONOPOLY

The most popular board game of all time actually started out as The Landlord's Game, conceived by Elizabeth Magie in 1904 in an effort to shine a light on economic imbalance. Instead, players reveled in amassing real estate empires and sending opponents into bankruptcy. While the game was circulated informally between friends, the first commercial version was produced 30 years after its initial development.

SHIRLEY TEMPLE DOLL

When "America's Little Darling" got her own doll in 1934, they flew off the store shelves. Within seven years, the Ideal Toy Company garnered $45 million in sales. While the dolls cost anywhere from $2 to $6 dollars at the time, one in mint condition would fetch close to $2,000 today.

VIEW-MASTER

Introduced at the 1939 New York's World Fair, the device that turns slides into three-dimensional images was originally sold in specialty photography stores. The first reels were of attractions around the country. It wasn't until 1951 that View-Master acquired the rights to Disney images, and sales skyrocketed.

After World War II, Army Men were made green to match the U.S. Army uniforms.

1940s

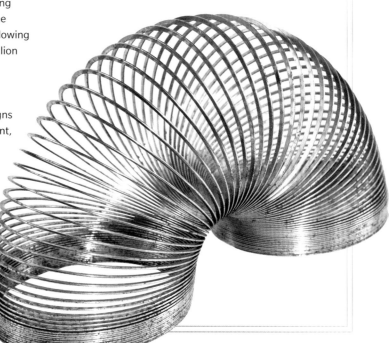

Sales didn't take off until after he partnered with his friend who renamed it Scrabble. Butts calculated the frequency of letters on the front page of *The New York Times* to determine how many points each letter should be worth.

SLINKY

The toy that's "fun for a girl or boy" hit the shelves of Gimbels department store in Philadelphia in 1945. Naval engineer Richard James was working on developing springs that would keep ship materials steady at sea. He accidentally knocked some samples off of a shelf and couldn't believe his eyes as the coils seemed to walk. Over 250 million Slinkys have been sold to date.

BUBBLES

Chemtoy, a Chicago company that sold cleaning supplies, began to bottle bubble solution in the early 1940s and children everywhere began blowing iridescent hollow spheres. Today, over 200 million bottles are sold each year.

MAGIC EIGHT BALL

Have you ever played with a Magic 8 Ball? "Signs point to yes." Created by the son of a clairvoyant, the fortune-telling device first got its pool ball–shape when Brunswick Billiards was looking for a fun promotional item. Today, the novelty toy is owned by Mattel, who sell more than a million each year.

SCRABBLE

Architect Alfred Mosher Butts created the board game in 1933, calling it Lexiko and then Criss Cross Words.

1950s

Barbie was invented at a time when most dolls were infants. ↘

BARBIE

Wanting a three-dimensional doll for her daughter to play with, Ruth Handler created the fashion model Barbie—an invention that went on to become the biggest selling fashion doll of all time! In an effort to boost girls' self-confidence, Barbie has grown to represent different races and occupations, while still maintaining her stellar style.

MR. POTATO HEAD

Before he became a movie star in 1995's *Toy Story*, Mr. Potato Head was created by inventor George Lerner, who thought that kids would play with food if that food had expressive faces. Mr. Potato Head earned Hasbro over $4 million in sales after just a few months on store shelves.

PEZ DISPENSER

Originally this candy was served in small tins until 1942 when the first PEZ dispenser was introduced. The first character-head dispenser (a Halloween Witch) was created in 1957.

PLAY-DOH

After Joe McVicker heard that modeling clay was too hard for children to manipulate with their hands, he took the malleable wallpaper cleaner his uncle had created in 1903 and sent it to school for kids to play with. It was a hit, and in 1956 the product was renamed Play-Doh.

1960s

100-watt incandescent light bulbs to bake mini cakes. To date, over 30 million units have been sold.

CHATTY CATHY

The pull-string talking doll from Mattel was the second most popular of the decade, just behind Barbie. Pull her "chatty ring" and she would deliver one of 11 phrases like, "Let's play school" or "I love you."

EASY-BAKE OVEN

The working toy oven was introduced by Kenner in 1963 and thrilled little bakers everywhere. It used two

ETCH A SKETCH

Created by electrician André Cassagnes, the aluminum-powder drawing toy sold 600,000 units in 1960. Like Mr. Potato Head, the Etch A Sketch was featured in the film *Toy Story*, which resulted in increased product sales.

G.I. JOE

The doll for boys, or action figure as Hasbro branded it, was created in the midst of the Cold War. G.I. Joe was modeled after the American soldiers of WWII and included a variety of equipment to play with.

LEGO

Now known as the "Toy of the Century" Lego bricks were invented in Denmark. The name is a mashup of *leg godt*, Danish for "play good." These small interlocking pieces inspire creativity—they can combine in over 500 ways.

Early versions of the Easy-Bake Oven were expensive: $15.95, the equivalent of $131.58 today.

1970s

PET ROCK

Marketed as a real live pet, the Pet Rock was created by Gary Dahl. Each rock was sold in a custom cardboard box with air holes. It took the purchasing public six months to realize that they were shelling out their hard-earned money for a rock, but by then the product had already made Dahl a millionaire.

RUBIK'S CUBE

Originally called the Magic Cube, Erno Rubik created this device in 1974 to explain 3D geometry. After Ideal Toy & Novelty Company renamed the puzzle Rubik's Cube, people all over the world wanted to solve it. Today it is still used widely for fun and also in competitions by "speedcubers."

SIMON

Invented by "the father of the video game," Ralph Baer, the electronic memory test was named after the schoolyard game Simon Says. The device creates a series of tones and lights that the player must repeat.

STRETCH ARMSTRONG

The corn syrup–filled action figure could stretch from its original size of 15 inches to over 4 feet!

1980s

CABBAGE PATCH KIDS

Created as a soft -sculpture by art student Xavier Roberts in 1976, the dolls were exhibited at arts and crafts shows in the Southeast. Two years later, Roberts began selling his sculptures with an "adoption" fee of $40. By 1983, over 3 million Cabbage Patch Kids had been adopted.

CARE BEARS

The multi-colored bears were originally created as greeting-card characters before becoming full plush teddy bears with their own TV specials.

MY LITTLE PONY

Introduced one year after My Pretty Pony, the new, smaller and more colorful ponies were much more successful—150 million were sold in the 1980s!

TEDDY RUXPIN

The animatronic children's toy shaped like a bear had an audiocassette player built in its back and would "read" to you as its eyes and mouth moved. Teddy Ruxpin was the best-selling toy of 1985–1986.

TRANSFORMERS

The media empire we know today began in 1984 with this toy. The Transformers product line features characters that morph from vehicles into robots.

My Little Pony is a shrunken version of My Pretty Pony, standing just 5 to 6 inches tall.

1990s

BEANIE BABIES

What made Beanie Babies different from other plushies on the market was the use of plastic pellets as stuffing. During the 90s, they were a huge fad and are considered by some to be "the world's first internet sensation."

BUZZ LIGHTYEAR

No one realized how popular 1995's *Toy Story* would be—certainly not manufacturer Thinkway Toys, who failed to produce enough of the space-hero action figures in time for Christmas. Parents everywhere were willing to go to infinity and beyond to get their hands on one.

FURBY

The 1998 toy from Tiger Electronics, a mix between a hamster and owl, was the hit toy of the holiday season. Each Furby spoke a language called "Furbish" and eventually used some English.

POWER RANGERS

Based on the live-action superhero TV show, Power Rangers dolls debuted in 1993. By 2001, the franchise had made more than $6 billion from toy sales.

TAMAGOTCHI

The hand-held digital pet was released in 1996 in Japan and worldwide the following year, and quickly became one of the most popular toys of the 90s. The keychain size was easy to carry and allowed you to interact with others who had Tamagotchi and create families in the world of the digital pets.

TEENAGE MUTANT NINJA TURTLES

TMNT was the first line of toys to generate billions of dollars. Original 1980s action figures of Leonardo, Michelangelo, Donatello and Raphael now fetch four figures. Cowabunga!

TICKLE ME ELMO

The toy of the 1996 holiday season, the furry red fella giggled when you squeezed his belly. Because the dolls were sold out just about everywhere, shoppers were arrested for fighting over them; others paid thousands of dollars to secondhand sellers.

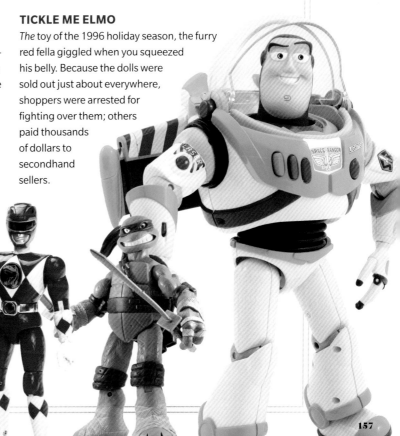

2000s

BRATZ DOLLS

Clad in tight-fitting outfits and donning heavy makeup, these dolls weren't loved by many parents—but it would seem that many bought them anyway. Debuting in 2001, over 125 million products were sold in the first five years.

RAZOR SCOOTER

Released in 2000, over 5 million were sold in the first six months alone! The compact folding scooter went on to become 2001's Toy of the Year.

ZHU ZHU PETS

The electronic hamsters that scurry about and even drive cars were a bit hit in 2009. And at $10 each, they were a bargain compared to other robotic pets.

BEYBLADES

These spinning tops, released in conjunction with an animated TV show, are a little more complex than those mentioned in the 1900s category. These Beys or Blades were customizable with interchangeable parts and used to battle opponents in plastic domes called Beystadiums. These tops topped $500 million in sales!

2010s

BABY SHARK OFFICIAL SONG DOLL

You've got to hand it to Pinkfong, a South Korean entertainment company. They took a song that's in the public domain (it's a camp song that dates back to the early 20th century) and turned it into the hottest toy of 2018. After their video featuring the earworm tune went viral, the company partnered with WowWee to release the baby shark doll—and kids and parents fell for it hook, line and sinker! Available for pre-sale on December 1 on Amazon at $17, the plush toy sold out in just two days.

ELSA DOLL

Based on the ice princess character from Disney's 2013 runaway hit *Frozen,* My First Disney Princess Frozen Snow Glow Elsa became one of the most popular toys of Christmas 2014.

FINGERLINGS

The tiny monkeys, unicorns and sloths that wrap around your finger and blow kisses and wink, were the brainchild of a 28-year-old brand manager. Shoppers waited in line for hours to snatch one of the hottest toys of 2017.

HATCHIMALS

These robotic toys seemed to fly off shelves as quickly as they were stocked. With an interactive furry toy that hatches from a plastic egg, the co-CEO of Spin Master (the company behind the toy), Anton Rabie, called it "the biggest phenom in decades." He's now worth $1.3 billion!

L.O.L. SURPRISE!

The number-one toy of 2017 comes in a dome-shaped case and contains 50 surprises that each have to be unwrapped. Thousands of unboxing videos of L.O.L. Surprise, which stands for Little Outrageous Little Surprise, popped up on YouTube, with one 13-minute video being viewed more than 13 million times.

TSUM TSUM

Referred to as "the new Beanie Baby," Disney had a new hit on their hands in 2014. In Japanese, *tsum* means stack, and that is what you are meant to do with these little, pellet-filled cuties.

AT HOME

WITH SANTA

WE INVITE JOLLY OLD ST. NICK INTO OUR LIVING ROOMS EVERY CHRISTMAS EVE. NOW IT'S TIME TO SEE WHERE HE AND MRS. CLAUS (AND THE ELVES) CALL HOME SWEET HOME.

Have you ever wondered where Santa sits down to read your letters? Or, where Mrs. Claus bakes her husband's favorite cookies? Yeah, we have too. But we don't have time to trek to the North Pole to visit. No worries: Zillow's got us covered. The real estate website has a listing for the 2,500-square-foot log-cabin that Santa built himself back in 1822. The home, which sits on a snowy, idyllic 25 acres of winter wonderland, underwent a renovation in 2017 during which many modern amenities were added.

1. FABULOUS FIREPLACE

After a long night of delivering presents to children all over the world, Santa comes home and curls up in front of the fireplace (made of floor-to-ceiling river rock) to relax. Adorning the mantel are 17th century German nutcrackers; hanging above the hearth, a 4K ultra HD smart TV, programmed with Christmas specials, of course!

2. MASTER SUITE

Mr. and Mrs. Claus slumber in quite the tranquil space! Their bedroom (one of three in the home) exudes a rustic feel, with its knotty pine woodwork, fresh greenery draping the window, cozy linens and plaid curtains. And if Santa needs a snack, his favorite (cookies and milk) is waiting for him on the nightstand.

3. SANTA'S OFFICE

It takes 364 days to prepare for his big night, so it's important for Santa to have a quiet place to plan it out and, of course, read all the letters he gets. His office is equipped with a typewriter, a telephone and maps. And when he needs a moment to unwind, there's a picture window to gaze out onto his winter wonderland.

4. DREAM KITCHEN

The kitchen is equipped with state-of-the-art appliances, including an oven with 12 cookie settings as well as hot cocoa on tap! The Nordic elements were inspired by the print of an apron that Santa got for Mrs. Claus while he was in Sweden. The French doors are perfect for when he wants to go visit the reindeer.

ELF

VILLAGE

5. A PLACE OF THEIR OWN
Early on, when Santa Claus first joined forces with the elves to make billions of toys each year, the little helpers knew they needed to live on site. (Migrating polar bears have been known to wreak havoc on commuters at the North Pole.) So the elves hand-crafted their very own village of 150-square-foot mini homes.

The tiny home trend has been sweeping the country lately, but the elves perfected the art of small-space living ages ago!

6. RUSTIC MINI CABIN

Each of the tiny elf homes is different. And that's good, since the owners have very different personalities. This rustic mini cabin made of hand-hewn logs really highlights the master craftsmanship of the elves, who helped one another in the building process. A wood-burning fireplace keeps the home toasty.

7. LUXE LOFT

The elves maximized space by keeping the living room and bathroom on the main floor and creating loft bedrooms, like this one. Knotty-pine walls and a reindeer-themed pillow and light fixtures add to the rustic vibe of this tiny bedroom—the perfect place to get a good night's sleep after a long day of toymaking.

8. PREP SPACE

When they're not busy making toys or tending to the reindeer, the elves love to entertain. This is the perfect space to prep hors d'oeuvres. Santa may have an insatiable sweet tooth, but some of his helpers have a more sophisticated palate: Their go-to snacks involve cheese platters and charcuterie boards.

9. PRACTICAL SOLUTIONS

They may be known for making toys, but the elves are pretty good at making furniture, too. The butcher-block desk and serving cart in this room were built by a very important elf—the Head of Toys, Woodworking Division. The bar cart is an especially useful piece, since counter space is so limited.

The frosty winter landscape is home to an enclave of elf houses, Santa's workshop, reindeer stables and a garage for the sleigh.

10. TINY FARMHOUSE

A decidedly different take on a little home, the icy blue shingles and chrome railings, portico and lighting on this petite farmhouse help it to meld seamlessly with the winter beauty all around it. Greenery on the banister and door lend a festive feel.

11. COMMUNAL TABLE

Santa's helpers are famous for their celebratory dinner parties, and the elf who lives in this house hosts many of them. The long table easily accommodates 10 for a sit-down dinner. The open-concept floor plan allows the host to mingle with guests, even while preparing the meal. Mrs. Claus has been known to stop by after dinner with a platter of just-out-of-the oven cookies during many a soiree.

12. PERFECT PANELS

Fixer Upper's Joanna Gaines isn't the only interior designer to favor shiplap. In fact, the elves have been using it for a very long time. Not only does it have a clean and orderly feel, but it's practical, too. According to Zillow: "Before it became a design choice, wood planks were the preferred siding for elf homes because of their ability to insulate from the cold, harsh climate."

13. BAMBOO BUNGALOW

This elf was looking to add a little zen to his life. And who could blame him? Meeting that Christmas Eve deadline can get pretty stressful! Crafted of bamboo, this petite bungalow, with its peace-sign wreath, is a warm and welcoming respite for all who enter.

14. TROPICAL TOUCH

Peacefully sleeping under a bamboo ceiling every night helps this elf to forget about the frozen tundra outside, even if just for a while. And don't worry about the little guy who lives here if there is a big snowstorm—bamboo is extremely durable.

15. MEDITATION SPACE

The flow between the elf's yoga studio (photo 16) and this meditation space creates a harmonious feng shui energy. The use of a Chinese incense burner and the addition of an energizing bonsai tree contribute to this tiny home's positive chi.

16. OM, SWEET OM

With space at a premium, this elf ingeniously managed to find room for a yoga studio. (When you are under 4 feet tall, you don't need that much space to do a downward-facing dog!) No need to travel far for a light post-workout lunch: The sushi bar is within reach.

A CHRISTMAS TO

SO MANY TRADITIONS, MOVIES, SONGS, TREATS AND DECORATIONS HELP MAKE THE SEASON MAGICAL. HERE ARE A FEW FAVORITES.

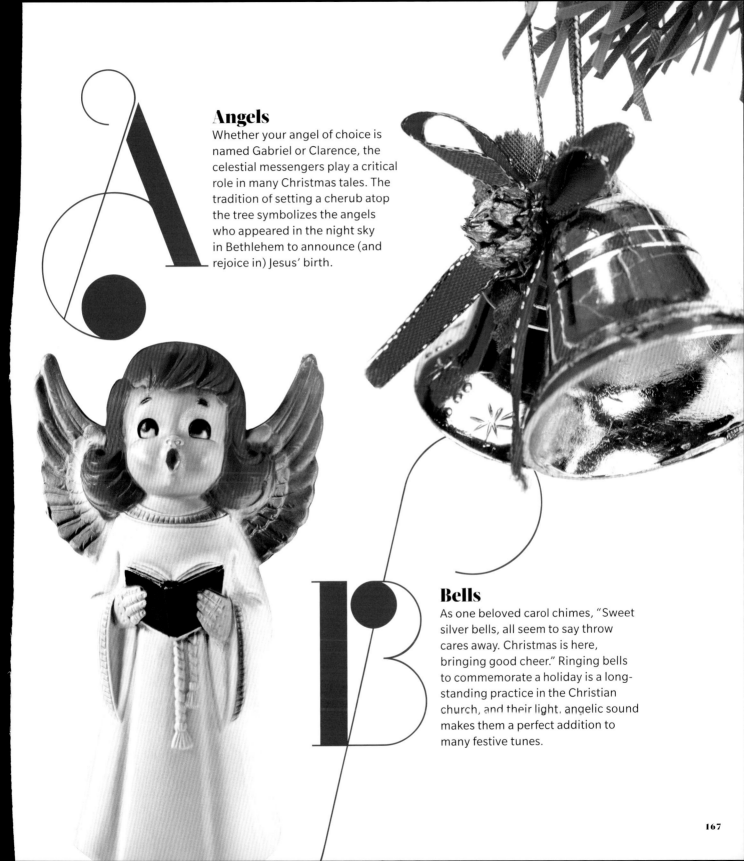

A

Angels

Whether your angel of choice is named Gabriel or Clarence, the celestial messengers play a critical role in many Christmas tales. The tradition of setting a cherub atop the tree symbolizes the angels who appeared in the night sky in Bethlehem to announce (and rejoice in) Jesus' birth.

B

Bells

As one beloved carol chimes, "Sweet silver bells, all seem to say throw cares away. Christmas is here, bringing good cheer." Ringing bells to commemorate a holiday is a long-standing practice in the Christian church, and their light, angelic sound makes them a perfect addition to many festive tunes.

C

Candy Canes

How do you quiet a cathedral full of chatty children? With candy, of course. As the story goes, a German choirmaster, seeking to quell some noisy youngsters, requested sugar sticks from a local candymaker. He asked for a crook on the end—a nod to the shepherds visiting baby Jesus—to justify their church distribution. Their connection to the Nativity made them popular Christmastime treats, and the minty confection remains a standby for tree-trimming and gift-giving today.

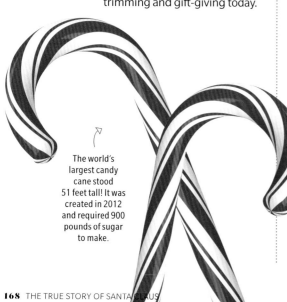

The world's largest candy cane stood 51 feet tall! It was created in 2012 and required 900 pounds of sugar to make.

D

Drummer Boy

The story of a poor Little Drummer Boy, summoned to Jesus' birth, offering the baby the only thing he had—the gift of music— was first recorded by the Trapp Family Singers (yes, *The Sound of Music* von Trapps!) in 1951. The song proved so popular, it's since been covered by everyone from Bing Crosby to Justin Bieber.

E

Eggnog

A festive favorite: Indiana University estimates that Americans drink 135 million pounds of eggnog each year. Though the concoction has been around since the Middle Ages, its association with Christmas can be traced to the 1700s. If you're looking for the right time to indulge in a creamy cup, we suggest Christmas Eve—it's National Eggnog Day!

F G H

Fruitcake

This dessert has long been a national punch line, considered an unpalatable (and unsightly) gift, likely from an out-of-touch great aunt. But after decades of abuse, the sweet snack is making a triumphant return. The vitriol can be traced back to a '60s-era Johnny Carson quip—"There is only one fruitcake in the entire world, and people keep sending it to each other, year after year"—that resonated enough to go viral, pre-Internet. Recently, though, national chains like Harry & David and Claxton Fruit Cake reported that sales are up. So this may just be the year of the fruitcake!

Gingerbread Man

Made all the more popular by its titular fairy tale and the beloved *Shrek* character, the figural biscuits took off when Queen Elizabeth I presented important guests with their very own gingertwin. While the Queen's cookies were surely impressive, they had nothing on the World's Largest Gingerbread Man. *The Guinness Book of World Records* lists it at 1,435.2 pounds—roughly the weight of seven adult American men!

Holly

This festive green flora is rife with symbolism: Its prickly leaves represent the crown of thorns that Jesus wore during the Crucifixion, while the red berries denote the drops of blood shed by Jesus from the thorns. Often paired with ivy (including in the popular holiday song), the two have been coupled since the days before Christianity, when both were used to decorate homes in winter.

> ## "Run, run as fast as you can! You can't catch me. I'm the Gingerbread Man!"
>
> THE GINGERBREAD MAN

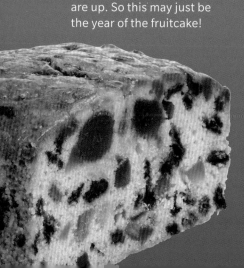

j o h

It's a Wonderful Life

Strange, isn't it? Each man's life touches so many others. The message of life's true meaning throughout this 1946 Christmas favorite resonates so strongly, it has spawned dozens of holiday-themed television shows, songs, games and books that adapt or parody the plot.

Jesus

As the angel told the shepherds in the field, "...unto you is born this day in the city of David, a Saviour which is Christ the Lord." The traditions, good tidings and sparkly tinsel make the season special, but as Linus touchingly reminds us in *A Charlie Brown Christmas*, the true meaning of Christmas lies in the birth of Jesus.

Kris Kringle

The man by any other name is just as jolly. Over millennia and across the globe, Santa Claus has gathered many monikers—St. Nick, Father Christmas, Pelznickel and, of course, Kris Kringle. "Kris" is an Americanized pronunciation of the South German Christkind, or "Christ Child," a relic from a time when the region believed baby Jesus was the bearer of gifts on Christmas Eve.

Lights

It turns out, Thomas Edison was a marketing maverick as much as an ingenious inventor. During the 1880 Christmas season, Edison decided to generate some PR for his incandescent light bulb by laying out eight miles of underground wire to power strings of lights around his laboratory in New Jersey. Commuters traveling between New Jersey and Philadelphia were so awestruck by the very first set of Christmas lights, one journalist dubbed Edison "The Enchanter."

Mistletoe

Couples and star-crossed lovers meeting under the mistletoe: It's a tale as old as time—or at least as old as the 18th-century English servants who likely founded the kissing tradition. In its original form, men would steal a kiss from any woman caught under the mistletoe—and refusal was considered to be bad luck for the coming year!

In 1900, it cost an estimated $300 to light a tree. That's the equivalent of $9,000 today!

North Pole

Santa's real workshop may be closed to tourists (imagine the distraction for the elves!), but you can plan your next vacation at an amusement park that sits within the Arctic Circle itself. A few miles north of Rovaniemi, Finland, in Santa Claus Village, guests can take reindeer rides, meet live snowmen and, of course, visit with St. Nick.

Popcorn String

Eat a piece, string a piece... and so it goes. Stringing popcorn for the tree is a tasty tradition dating all the way back to the first Christmas trees in Germany. The secret to the perfect string? Use waxed dental floss and day-old popcorn to avoid breaks.

The Queen's Christmas Message

For some 60 years, Queen Elizabeth II has delivered a royal Christmas greeting to her citizens in the Commonwealth of Nations. The speech, a mix of personal insights and the news stories of the year, is broadcast on TV, on radio and online. The tradition started with her father, George V, in 1932, but the public's relationship with the monarchy really changed in 1957. Broadcast live on television for the first time, the Queen spoke directly to her viewers around the globe: "I very much hope that this new medium will make my Christmas message more personal and direct," she said, "at least for a few minutes, I welcome you to the peace of my own home."

Ornaments

From German blown glass to cartoon critters, every ornament tells a story— and they create a tree's personality. Check out the Christmas Ornament Calculator at santasquarters. com to figure out how many baubles to put on your tree.

Robin

The red-breasted birds have long been associated with Christmastime, but what's the connection? In the Victorian Era, British Royal Mail postmen wore bright red uniforms. The regal color (it's linked to the flag and royal family) earned them the nickname "robins." Families eagerly awaited the arrival of the "robin" who delivered their Christmas cards. Some card illustrators began drawing an actual robin carrying Christmas cards in his beak. It started as a joke, but the robin soon became a symbol of Christmas.

Sugar Plum Fairy

The Nutcracker ballet is a staple of the Christmas season. Act II stars the prima ballerina as the Sugar Plum Fairy—ruler of the Land of Sweets—who celebrates the arrival of Clara and the Nutcracker Prince with a lavish fete in her Candy Castle and bids them farewell with a dazzling *pas de deux*.

Twelve Days of Christmas

A dozen days of Christmas means a dozen days of presents—imagine that credit card bill? According to the PNC Christmas Price Index, an entire set of presents from the 12 Days of Christmas would have set customers back $34,558.65 in 2017. Oh, and if you've ever thought to ask your true love for the five gold rings offered up in this carol, you may want to think again! Evidence suggests the song may actually refer to the yellow rings around a pheasant's neck—in keeping with the avian theme of days one through seven—and not, as many assume, the precious-metal band.

A MERRY CHRISTMAS TO YOU

"Up on the Housetop"

This song, written by Benjamin Hanby in 1864, is the second-oldest secular Christmas song (beat out only by "Jingle Bells," which was written seven years earlier and was originally a Thanksgiving song!). The ditty had a resurgence when, in 2005, *American Idol* alum Kimberley Locke's cover catapulted to the No. 1 spot on the *Billboard* Adult Contemporary chart—where it stayed for four consecutive weeks!

A Very (Insert TV Show Family) Christmas

From the Bradys in 1988 to *Full House*'s Tanners in 1992 to the Griffins of *Family Guy* in 2001 and the cast of *Glee* in 2010, this quintessential title for holiday sitcom specials always sets the mood for the season. Characters are reunited, songs are sung, someone stops by dressed as Santa Claus and, for a single episode, all is right in TV land—except, of course, on *Family Guy*!

Wisconsin's Santa's Wreath Co. makes 25,000 of its fresh balsam decorations each year, using a cement mixer to paint 80,000 pine cones.

Wreath

Both a decorative cousin of the Christmas Tree and symbolic of Christ's suffering—evergreen represents eternal life—hanging wreaths may have started in ancient Rome as a sign of victory after battle.

Xmas

While many assume "Xmas" to be a simple abbreviation for "Christmas," the *X* has actually been a stand-in for "Christ" for more than 1,000 years! The word comes from a coupling of the Greek letter chi (*X*, the first letter in *Christos*, the Greek word for "Christ") and *mas*, an Old English word for "mass."

Yule Log

Imagine, in a world filled with Netflix bingeing and endless entertainment options, green-lighting a television program consisting solely of Christmas tunes and a burning log. In 1966, when the Yule Log program first aired on WPIX—catering to a New York City audience, who largely had no fireplace to cozy up next to—it was a hit. Surprisingly, despite an 11-year hiatus in the '90s, the three-hour special continues to air today.

The first made-for-TV Yule Log was filmed at Gracie Mansion (home of New York City's mayor).

Zwetschgenmännchen

The German word for "Plum People," these are dried fruit figures that traditionally are made at Christmas, going back to 1790. Standing about 6 inches tall, with figs for bodies, dried plums for arms, raisins for hands, and painted walnuts for heads, the little figures are dressed in scraps of material as everything from chimney sweeps to grandmothers. A symbol of good luck in Germany, it's said: "You will never be without gold and happiness, if you have a prune person in your house."

SANTA

They have some pretty big boots to fill. Santa schools around the world train men for the job.

SCHOOL

ST. NICK DOESN'T ALLOW JUST ANYONE TO FILL IN FOR HIM AT THE MALL—EXTENSIVE TRAINING IS REQUIRED.

It's no surprise that Santa needs a little help—especially in the weeks leading up to his big trip around the globe. He's busy checking his list (twice, in case you haven't heard!), as well as overseeing the elves' toy production and making sure his reindeer are in tip-top flying shape. So where does the Big Guy go for assistance? He looks to graduates from academies around the world that have been preparing students to play Santa Claus, some since the early 20th century.

Every year, hordes of facsimile Father Christmases sign up for comprehensive training at these schools. After all, you need more than just the furry red suit and a pair of black boots. There is a lot to learn to be a stand-in for Santa. There are standards to uphold and rules to follow. Let's take a look at what students learn at the most famous of the Santa schools.

"He errs who thinks Santa enters through the chimney. Santa enters through the heart."

CHARLES W. HOWARD

The Ivy League of Santa Schools

The longest continuously running St. Nick training facility is the Charles W. Howard Santa Claus School. Now located in Midland, Michigan, the "Harvard of Santa Schools" was founded in New York in 1937 by Charles W. Howard. (He went on to play Santa in the Macy's Thanksgiving Day Parade from 1948 through 1965.)

Howard was inspired to create the school after coming across too many second-rate Santa stand-ins while visiting department stores. The poor grooming and bad behavior he witnessed was not, in Howard's opinion, living up to the responsibility of wearing the suit. "There was a need for better Santas," the school's current dean, Tom Valent, explained to *National Geographic* in 2016. "Some of the Santa characters were apparently pretty rough, smoking and drinking."

So Howard set out to change things for the better, striving to ensure that every child encountering the legendary figure would leave feeling that signature Santa magic. Mission accomplished—83 years later, the school has graduated more than 5,000 jolly old elves, and its stellar reputation keeps veterans coming back for the latest training. "After Christmas, when it's a bit of a letdown, you think, 'I can't wait to go to Midland again,'" student Charles Stervinou told the *Lansing State Journal* in 2015. "You can always learn something new here. People think Santa school is a joke. It's not."

Santa Jerry Owens agrees. As a friend once told him: "The day that you stop wanting to learn how to be a better Santa Claus is the day you need to hang up the suit and quit."

Lesson Plan

Wannabe Clauses are required to train in a variety of subjects. "Know who you are," Valent told an assembly of Santas, according to CNN. "Know your legend. Know where you came from." To that end, topics studied include the history of St. Nicholas, the North Pole, Christmas carols, toymaking and reindeer behavior (including meeting with live reindeer!)

Knowledge is key, but equally important is looking, acting and sounding the part, not just for gigs at department stores, but also for TV and radio interviews. Jerry Givens, a retiree from Albany, Indiana, who's played Santa for years, takes his role very seriously. "It's not me, it's the character I portray. I'm an actor. My job is to make you believe again," he said in 2015. One way he accomplishes that goal is with a makeup kit made specifically for Santa stand-ins. Givens uses the makeup, developed by a circus clown ("Who else knows more about men's makeup?"), to teach other students how "to take the shine off their foreheads with powder, pink up their cheeks with rouge, and add stardust to their beards with hairspray that contains glitter," according to the *Lansing State Journal*.

A Hairy Subject

Who wears a beard that's long and white? Over 300 students in Charles W. Howard's Class of 2019! And beard maintenance is a big deal. The industry standard is real whiskers, but wigs can be purchased and applied at school. Santa must be prepared for the tug test, made popular by the film *Miracle on 34th Street* in 1947. If a child can see the string of a false beard, you'll lose credibility quicker than an eager child can rip open a present on Christmas morning. And those who don't need a wig are taught how to properly bleach their beards and hair. (FYI: It's a gradual process to avoid burning the hair!)

Other tricks of the transformation trade, according to John Wetters, a burly former Santa for the Chicago Blackhawks: "Don't trim your eyebrows; leave them nice and bushy" and "wrinkles help—they give you a nice, frosty look."

One of the secrets that students learn at Santa school: Adding peppermint oil to your beard will make it smell magical!

Vocal exercises are performed at the Charles W. Howard school to help Santas-in-training perfect the signature Santa laugh.

Communication Is Key

Another lesson: mastering the "Ho Ho Ho." It's harder than you might think! "You have to do it mild," Valent explained. "It's got to be a laugh."

Basic sign language is also taught during the three-day session. "It's important to be able to spread Christmas cheer to all children," a Santa named Bill told Reuters.

A golden rule for all Santa stand-ins is to never make a promise. "You get 'I just want my mom and dad to get back together,' or 'I want Grandma to get better.' Those are tough," says Alan Spencer, a Santa based in New England. "You never make any promises, but kids just want to talk about the tough stuff, so you listen." Santa Greg Gilpin shares his strategy for such instances: He reminds the children that Santa's magic is in toys.

Physical Demands

Sure, Santa Claus is expected to be plump, but that doesn't mean he shouldn't be fit. In fact, it's a requirement for the job. The reality is that Santa is not just sitting on a throne all day, posing for photos and listening to kids' wish lists. "You have to get into a full squat to talk to kids," Spencer told Reebok.com. "It's exhausting."

Students at the Howard School engage in yoga, stretching and breathing exercises with a fitness teacher to stay limber. And that can come in handy, because as Santa Claus, you never know what's going to be thrown your way.

Case in point: "I was sitting there, and they filed the children in," Owens revealed to Indiana's *News and Tribune*. "They had assigned spots on the floor, but this one young girl, she couldn't hold back her excitement, and she shot out of line and ran straight for me in the chair, and within six feet away from me, she became airborne. Her arms were wide open, and I'm thinking, 'Oh my God, I can't let her fall.' So I reached out and I grabbed her, and she hugged me real tight and looked at me, and said 'Santa?' I said, 'Yes?' And she said, 'I love you.' At that point I knew: This was something I needed to do." And luckily, he was prepared for the catch!

The Business of Being Santa

This is not a low-cost activity. A quality suit can cost upward of $600 and a custom one, around $2,000.

A session at the Charles W. Howard school begins with an open house on Wednesday night, followed by class from 8:30 a.m. to 9 p.m. on Thursday, Friday and Saturday.

Charles W. Howard was the Macy's Thanksgiving Day Parade Santa from 1948 to 1965 and served as a "Santa consultant" for 1947's *Miracle on 34th Street*.

Santa Greg Gilpin

A quality, custom-made suit can cost up to $2,000.

A fitted beard will set you back $1,000, and a good pair of leather boots? That'll be $700. And that's all before incidentals like dry-cleaning and makeup—not to mention the $525 tuition. The Howard school understands this, and that's why it also offers lessons in marketing, accounting and taxes. "It's pretty expensive, but everybody does it because they enjoy it," says Gilpin. "You love the looks on the kids' faces when they walk into the room and gasp 'It's Santa!'"

Most important, the school trains Santa stand-ins to live with Christmas in their hearts. That is what will truly make children believe. "We cover a lot," Valent notes, but the most valuable lesson of all? "We teach the spirit of Christmas...

we get their Santa spirit growing so it will continue throughout the year."

Santas find their Christmas calling in many ways. Some are hoping to bring new meaning to their days after retirement; others are looking for a foray into the professional world of play. No matter what brings each of them to class, one thing is clear: Santa schools exist because each potential Father Christmas embraces the joy and kindness Santa Claus stands for. "Santa reflects all the good qualities that we want everyone to have—he gives gifts and love and compassion and cares for children," says Gilpin. "It's important to me that I portray him in a way that treats him with the utmost respect."

SANTAS BY THE SLEiGHFUL

COLLECTORS ACROSS GENERATIONS KEEP THE SPIRIT OF SANTA ALIVE ALL YEAR.

"It's a funny thing; if you're feeling down, you can come sit in the Santa Claus room," Heather Shayne says.

C hristmas and Santa were always special to me," confesses Nancy Laier, who has been collecting Santas since the 1960s. And he would have to be— Laier, who resides in a small home, just west of Eustis, Nebraska—decorates her home year-round with about 9,000 Santas. But you never forget your first. For Laier, it was won at a Pizza Hut prize drawing in the 1960s.

Dolph Gotelli, known as "Father Christmas," and a professor emeritus of design at the University of California, Davis, who specializes in Victorian Era Santa collections, started collecting when he was 7 years old. "It was after Christmas during [World War II], and my mother stopped at a Woolworth Five and Dime. There was a little Santa Claus, half price, maybe a dollar, and that was my first Santa."

"When I started looking for vintage [Santa mugs], I told myself 'I have to have every one of them!'" collector Heather Shayne says. Today, she has more than 425.

183

"Santa in red isn't as valuable, but in blue or purple, that's what people want," explains Dolph Gotelli.

Santa-themed toys and games were popular gifts in the late 19th and early 20th century.

While some collections lose popularity, toys and games are still a valuable find.

Dolph Gotelli has hundreds of Victorian-era Santa die-cuts. "The printing process, the colors, the layers and embossing were so beautiful," he says.

RING MY NOSE! THE NEW SANTA CLAUS WALL QUOITS

Dolph Gotelli tracked this loofah Santa—first spotted in a small store in England—around the world before he finally landed it at a local doll show in California.

For Heather Shayne, it was a set of vintage-style mugs from Pier 1 in 2015 that set off a love for '50s-era Santa collectibles.

The collections of these three individuals span generations, but their collective passion is universal.

Years of Yuletide

As prices rise in the internet era, true collectors say the love of the hunt makes it all worthwhile. Even after selling much of his collection in 2019, Gotelli admits: "If you're a collector, it's an addiction. There's no way I would ever get rid of everything!" Now, it's about finding "the rarest of the rare," he says, and sharing these pieces of history with generations to come—whether near, like the Christmas museum he opened in his Sacramento home in the '80s, or far, like the countless exhibits he's curated for museums and department stores around the nation.

Laier opens her home to all who'd like the Santa experience. "I had over 100 people come in this year to see [the Santas] before and after Christmas—even schools bring their pupils to see them."

Shayne's "grand opening" for her "Christmas room" started out as a joke, but now visits are regularly requested. "It's like Christmas sucks you in and takes you back to the past. I don't think you could re-create that with the new stuff," she says.

"There's a benefit for these [vintage pieces] to be shown," Gotelli adds. "Kids today, they still have the stockings and the gifts, but the department store Santas are starting to disappear—he's a cultural icon that I don't want to see fade away."

Heather Shayne's Santa collection started with these Pier 1 mugs.

A

Advertisements, Santa in, 20, 21, 115, 126–133
Albert (Prince Consort of Queen Victoria), 70, 74
Alcott, Louisa May, 31
Allen, Tim (movie Santa), 102
Amish sugar cookies, 87
Anderson, Alexander (artist), 112, 113
Angels, 167
Antlers, 42
Asner, Ed (movie Santa), 107
Attenborough, Richard (movie Santa), 105
Australia, Christmas traditions in, 90, 91
Austria, Christmas traditions in, 91

B

Babbo Natale (Italian Santa), 89, 94
Baum, L. Frank, 42
Bells, 167
Bon Velhinho (Brazilian Santa), 91
Books, Santa and Mrs. Claus featured in, 29, 140–143
Brazil
    Christmas traditions in, 90, 91
    decorated tree, 75
Brothers Grimm, 33, 35

C

Call, John (movie Santa), 108
Candy canes, 168
Can Reindeer Fly? The Science of Christmas (Highfield), 45
Charles W. Howard Santa Claus School, 178–181
Children
    books for, 29, 141–143
    letters written by. *See* Letters, from children
    naughty and nice lists of, 14, 24, 35, 63
    Santa's message to, 89
    visiting Santa in stores/malls, 64–67
Chimneys
    Santa's entrance via, 50–51
    stockings hung by, 60
China, Christmas traditions in, 92
Christkind, 91, 92, 93, 170
Christmas cards. *See* Holiday greetings cards
Christmas Eve visits, by Santa
    customs associated with, 48–57
    science and magic of, 44–47
    snacks for, 87
    tracking, 45
Christmas message
    from Queen of England, 172
    from Santa to children, 89

Christmas traditions, 166–173
    decorated trees, 70–75
    greetings cards. *See* Holiday greetings cards
    hanging stockings, 60–63
    international, 88–97
    origins of, 17
Christmas trees, 70–75
    types best suited for, 72–73
    worldwide examples, 75
Coal, for naughty children, 63
Cole, Sir Henry, 77, 79
Collections/Collectors, of Santa items, 182–185
Collins, Ace, 77
Commercialization, of Santa, 20, 21, 58–59, 115,
        126–133, 142
CONAD (Continental Air Defense Command), 45
Cookie traditions, 84–87
Costumes, for Santas, 181

D

Ded Moroz (Russian Santa), 95–96, 97
Department stores, visiting Santa in, 64–67
"Der Weinachtsmann" (German Santa), 93
Druids, 71
Drummer boy, 168

E

Edgar, James, 67
Edible gifts, in European pagan traditions, 85
Eggnog, 168
Elf (movie), 32
Elf Village houses, 162–165
Elizabeth II (Queen of England), 172
Elves
    as Santa's helpers, history of, 20, 30–37
    homes of, 162–165
    Icelandic Yule Lads, 35
    in movies, 32, 34–37
    in Norse mythology, 33, 95, 97, 114
    Kringle family of, 35
    workshop of, 32–33
"The Elves and the Shoemaker" (Grimm folktale), 35
emailsanta.com, 57
England, Christmas traditions in, 92–93
"Even a Miracle Needs a Hand" (song), 120
Evergreen wreaths, 174

F

Father Christmas
    in English tradition, 92–93

in German tradition, 93

international names/images for, 7, 88–97

Father Frost (Russian/Ukrainian Santas), 87, 95–96

Fattigmann (cookie), 87

Finland, Christmas traditions in, 88, 93

Folktales, elves depicted in, 33, 35

France

Christmas traditions in, 93

decorated tree, 75

Frosty the Snowman (TV special), 121

Fruitcake, 169

G

Generosity, in cookie tradition origins, 85, 87

Germany

Christmas traditions in, 93

decorated tree, 75

Giamatti, Paul (movie Santa), 104

Gillen, Jeff (movie Santa), 110

Gingerbread/Gingerbread man (cookies), 87, 169

Gnomes. *See* Elves

Godey's Lady's Book, 35, 36

Greetings cards. *See* Holiday greetings cards

Guinness beer, for Santa, 87

Gwenn, Edmund (movie Santa), 101

H

Hall Brothers (postcard printing company), 79

Hallmark greetings cards, 79

Santa images on (1910–2017), 80–83

Hanks, Tom (movie Santa), 103

Harper's Weekly

poem about elves in, 35

Santa images in, 17, 20, 51, 53, 55

Hay, in Christmas traditions, 63, 85, 95, 97

"Here Comes Santa Claus" (song), 138

Highfield, Roger, 45

Hogan, Hulk (movie Santa), 109

Holiday greetings cards, 76–79

Santa images on (1910–2017), 80–83

statistics on, 79

Holiday music/songs

about Santa, 43, 54, 120, 134–139, 173, 174

best-selling singles, 138–139

Holiday season, start of, 59

Holiday TV specials

cartoons/animations, 43, 116–123

sitcoms, 174

Yule Log program, 175

Holly, 169

Horsley, John Callcott (artist), 77

Hoteiosho (Buddhist monk), 95

How the Grinch Stole Christmas (TV special), 118

Huddleston, David (movie Santa), 107

I

Iceland, Christmas traditions in, 93–94

"I'm Sending a Letter to Santa Claus" (song), 55

Ireland, Christmas traditions in, 94

Irving, Washington, 14, 17, 47, 141

"I Saw Mommy Kissing Santa Claus" (song), 138–139

Italy

Christmas traditions in, 89, 94

decorated trees, 75

It's a Wonderful Life (movie), 74, 169

Ivory, Edward (movie Santa), 108

J

Japan

Christmas traditions in, 94–95, 96

decorated tree, 75

Jesus Christ, 170

"Jingle Bells" (song), 174

Jólakötturinn (Yule Cat), 94

Joulupukki (Finnish Santa), 88, 93

Julbocken (Christmas goat), 97

Jultomten (Swedish Santa), 89, 95, 97

K

A Knickerbocker's History of New York (Irving), 14, 17, 51, 141

Krampus (Austrian monster), 91

Kringle, Kris (Santa pseudonym), 101

L

Lange, Artie (movie Santa), 111

"The Legend of Christmas" (tale), 23

Letters, from children

prompting newspaper editorial, 20, 142, 143

to Santa, 52–57, 76, 93

Leyendecker, J.C. (illustrator), 17, 22, 114–115

The Life and Adventures of Santa Claus (Baum), 42

Lights, 171

Lill's Travel in Santa Claus Land and Other Stories (Towne, May & Farman), 29

Livingston, Henry, Jr., 17

Lomen, Carl ("Reindeer King"), 42

Lorenzetti, Ambroglio (artist), 112, 113

Los Reyes Magos (Three Kings), 96–97

Luther, Martin, 14, 70, 73
Lynn, Vera, 55

M

Macy's Thanksgiving Day Parade, 58–59
Mince pies, 87
Miracle on 34th Street (movie), 7, 59, 101, 105, 178, 181
Mistletoe, 171
Moore, Clement C., 14, 17–18, 33, 41–42, 51, 114, 141
Movies
    Christmas trees depicted in, 74
    elves portrayed in, 32, 34–37
    Mrs. Claus portrayed in, 26–29
    Santa portrayed in, 101–111
Mrs. Claus, 24–29
    first mention of, 23
    hometown of, 22–23
    movie portrayals of, 26–29
    pseudonyms for, 29
Music. *See* Holiday music/songs

N

Nast, Thomas (cartoonist), 17, 18–20, 33, 51, 52, 53, 55, 112, 113–114
Naughty and Nice lists
    children, 14, 35, 63
    Santa portrayals, 100–111
The Netherlands
    Christmas traditions in, 94, 95
    decorated tree, 75
New York *Sun*, editorial on Santa Claus, 20, 142, 143
Nigeria, Christmas traditions in, 95
NORAD (North American Aerospace Defense Command), 45
noradsanta.org, 45
Norse mythology
    elves in, 33, 95, 97, 114
    Odin's horse in, 63, 85
North Pole, 20, 171
    dwellings at, 160–165
    Elves' workshop, 32–33
    zip code for, 57
The Nutcracker ballet, 173
    tree ornaments, 72
Nyström, Jenny (artist), 114

O

O'Hanlon, Virginia, 142, 143
Ornaments, 172
    trees decorated with, 70–75

P

Pan de Pascua (bread), 87
Papa Noel (Brazilian Santa), 91
Pepparkakor (cookie), 87
Père Noël/Papa Noël (French Santa), 92, 93
Pfeffernuss (cookie), 87
Pintard, John, 14, 17
Plum People (Zwetschgenmännchen), 175
PNC Christmas Price Index, 173
"Poop" log, 91
Popcorn string, 172
Pop culture, Mrs. Claus in, 26–29
Pop culture, Santa in, 98–143
    artists' renderings, 16, 17–21, 50, 51, 53, 55, 60, 112–115
    books, 42, 140–143
    characters imitating, 114–125
    memorabilia collections, 182–185
    movie portrayals, 101–111
    product advertisements, 20, 21, 115, 126–133
    songs, 43, 54, 120, 134–139, 173, 174
    TV specials. *See* Holiday TV specials
Postage stamps, 22
Prang, Louis, 79
Product advertisements, Santa in, 20, 21, 115, 126–133

Q

The Queen's Christmas Message, 172

R

Ra (Egyptian sun god), 71
Rees, James, 23
Reindeer, 38–43
    as Kris Kringle's "next of kin," 101
    in Moore poem, 15, 18, 41–42
    Santa's sleigh and, 44–45
Risalamande (snack), 87
Robin (bird), 173
Rockwell, Norman, 17, 114–115
Rudolf the Red–Nosed reindeer (TV special), 25, 43, 119
Russell, Kurt (movie Santa), 106
Russia, Christmas traditions in, 95–96

S

St. Nicholas, 12, 13
    descriptions/images of, 14, 17, 51, 112–114
    in European Christmas traditions, 91, 93, 94, 95, 97
    legend of/stories associated with, 63, 85
St. Nicholas Day (December 6), 14, 17, 87, 91, 93, 94, 95, 97

Samichlaus (Swiss Santa), 97
Sandbakelse (cookie), 87
San Nioclàs/Daidí na Nollag (Irish Santa), 94
"Santa Baby" (song), 139
santaclassics.com, 115
Santa Claus
    home of, 160–161
    in pop culture. *See* Pop culture, Santa in
    international names for, 7, 88–97
    origins of, 8–21
    wife of, 22–29
"Santa Claus Is Comin' to Town" (song), 137
Santa Claus Is Comin' to Town (TV special), 35, 122
Santa Claus Village, Finland, 171
Santa's sleigh, tracking by NORAD, 45
Santa's Wreath Co., 174
santatracker.google.com, 45
Saturday Evening Post, Santa images in, 14, 22, 115
Saturnalia (Roman midwinter feast), 71
Schools, for Santa training, 176–181
Sheng dan Lao ren (Chinese Santa), 92
Sherry, for Santa, 87
Shopping malls, visiting Santa in, 64–67
Shoup, Col. Harry, 45
Sinterklaas (Dutch Santa), 12–14, 89, 95
Snacks for Santa
    history of, 85, 87
    international versions, 86–87
Snegurochka/Snow Maiden (Santa's granddaughter),
    95, 96
Spain, Christmas traditions in, 96–97
Springerle (cookie), 87
Stockings, tradition of hanging, 60–63
Stories Behind the Great Traditions of Christmas
    (Collins), 77
Sugar Plum Fairy, 173
The Sun, editorial on Santa Claus, 20, 142, 143
Sundblom, Haddon (artist), 20, 115, 129, 131
Svyatyy Mykolay (Ukrainian Santa), 97
Sweden, Christmas traditions in, 89, 95, 97
Switzerland, Christmas traditions in, 97

T
Television. *See* Holiday TV specials
Thankfulness, in cookie tradition origins, 85, 87
Thornton, Billy Bob (movie Santa), 110
Tió de Nadal (Christmas log), 97
Toymaker, Santa as, 20
Toys
    as Christmas tree decorations, 72

most desired, by decade (1900s–2010s), 146–159
Tracking Santa's sleigh, 45
Training to be Santa, 176–181
Trees, customs/celebrations associated with, 70–71.
    See also Christmas trees
" 'Twas the Night Before Christmas" (first line).
    See "A Visit from St. Nicholas" (poem)
'Twas the Night Before Christmas (TV special), 120
"Twelve Days of Christmas" (song), 173

U
Ukraine, Christmas traditions in, 97
United States
    decorated trees in, 72–73, 75
    holiday greetings cards and, 79
    letters to Santa in, 55, 57
    tracking Santa's sleigh, 45
"Up on the Housetop" (song), 174

V
Vehicles, for Santa's Christmas Eve visits, 46–47
Victoria (Queen of England), 70, 74
Vintage Santas, collecting, 182–185
"A Visit from St. Nicholas" (poem), 15, 17–18, 33, 41–42,
    51, 115, 141

W
Wheeler, Ed (photographer), 115
Wine, for Santa, 87
"The Wonders of Santa Claus" (poem), 35
Wreaths, 174
Wyeth, N.C. (artist), 113, 114

X
Xmas, meaning of, 175
Xmas pickle, legend of, 97

Y
The Year Without a Santa Claus (TV special), 123
Yule Cat (Jólakötturinn), 94
Yule Goat (Finnish), 93–94
Yule Lads (Icelandic Christmas tradition), 35, 93, 93–94
Yule log, 47, 175

Z
Zillow listing, for home of Santa and Mrs. Claus,
    160–161
Zip code, for Santa, 57
Zwarte Piet (Black Peter), 12–14
Zwetschgenmännchen (Plum People), 175

COVER Tom Newsom/Mendola Art **FRONT FLAP** Courtesy of the U.S. Postal Service **2–3** Yuganov Konstantin/Shutterstock **4–5** Shutterstock; Jamie Grill/Getty Images; Courtesy of Fox Entertainment; nito/Shutterstock; New Line/Everett Collection; Yvonne Hemsey/Getty Images; Courtesy of ABC **6–7** loridambrosio/Getty Images **8–9** Transcendental Graphics/Getty Images **10–11** Jose Luis Pelaez/Getty Images **12–13** Heritage Images/Getty Images; World Archive/Alamy Stock Photo **14–15** Getty Images; Courtesy of the Library of Congress; The New York Historical Society/Getty Images; WikiMedia Commons **16–17** Curtis Publishing/Saturday Evening Post; Courtesy of the Hallmark Archives, Hallmark Cards, Inc., Kansas City, Missouri, USA; Courtesy of the Library of Congress; GL Archive/Alamy Stock Photo **18–19** Sarin Images/Granger (2) **20–21** Courtesy of the U.S. Postal Service; The Advertising Archives/Alamy Stock Photo **22–23** WikiMedia Commons **24–25** Pictures Now/Alamy Stock Photo; The History Collection/Alamy Stock Photo **26–27** Columbia Pictures/Everett Collection; Courtesy of ABC; Hallmark Entertainment/Everett Collection; Ed Araquel/Lifetime Television/Everett Collection; TriStar Pictures/Everett Collection; PhotoFest **28–29** PictureLux/The Hollywood Archive/Alamy Stock Photo; Allstar Picture Library/Alamy Stock Photo **30–31** Hulton Archive/Getty Images **32–33** New Line/Everett Collection **34–35** NBC/Getty Images; Courtesy of ABC **36–37** Moviestore Collection Ltd./Alamy Stock Photo; Collection Christophel/Alamy Stock Photo; Warner Bros./Everett Collection **38–39** Michel Tcherevkoff/Getty Images **40–41** GraphicaArtis/Getty Images **42–43** WikiMedia Commons (2); AndreyTTL/Getty Images; GraphicaArtis/Getty Images; Buena Vista Pictures/Everett Collection **44–45** Ramberg/Getty Images; robert hyrons/Alamy Stock Photo **46–47** Buyenlarge/Getty Images; bilwissedition Ltd. & Co. KG/Alamy Stock Photo; This Old Postcard/Alamy Stock Photo; Print Collector/Getty Images; WikiMedia Commons; Keith Corrigan/Alamy Stock Photo **48–49** Per Breiehagen/Getty Images **50–51** duncan1890/Getty Images; SunFlowerStudio/Alamy Stock Photo; Nawrocki/ClassicStock/Getty Images; Sheridan Libraries/Levy/Gado/Getty Images **52–53** Lanmas/Alamy Stock Photo; North Wind Picture Archives/Alamy Stock Photo **54–55** lisegagne/Getty Images **56–57** Allan Swart/Alamy Stock Photo; Courtesy of santaclausmuseum.org; visualspace/Getty Images **58–59** NBC/Getty Images; Bettmann/Getty Images; New York Daily News Archive/Getty Images; Bettmann/Getty Images **60–61** Bettmann/Getty Images; avid_creative/Getty Images **62–63** Walt Disney Home Video/Everett Collection; Fine Art Photographic/Getty Images; Picture Post/Getty Images; Everett Collection; Transcendental Graphics/Getty Images; clintspencer/Getty Images **64–65** Ralph Morse/Getty Images; ROBYN BECK/Getty Images; National Film Board of Canada/Getty Images; WikiMedia Commons; Chris Ware/Getty Images; Carl Court/Getty Images **66–67** Everett Collection; Lambert/Getty Images; Michael Ochs Archives/Getty Images; Neilson Barnard/Getty Images; Reg Innell/Getty Images; FREDERIC J. BROWN/Getty Images; Bettmann/Getty Images (2); Underwood Archives/Getty Images **68–69** Per Breiehagen/Getty Images **70–71** Hulton Archive/Getty Images (2); GraphicaArtis/Getty Images **72–73** Print Collector/Getty Images; Darren McCollester/Getty Images; MCNY/Gottscho-Schleisner/Getty Images; picture alliance/Getty Images; Portland Press Herald/Getty Images; Maxfocus/Getty Images; Jessica Kirk/Getty Images; IrisImages/Getty Images; Istvan Balogh/Getty Images **74–75** Silver Screen Collection/Getty Images; Everett Collection (3); Columbia/Everett Collection; Everett Collection; Valerio Mei/Alamy Stock Photo; Ranimiro Lotufo Neto/Alamy Stock Photo; Ball Miwako/Alamy Stock Photo; mauritius images GmbH/Alamy Stock Photo; blickwinkel/Alamy Stock Photo; Xinhua/Alamy Stock Photo; Edwin Remsberg/Alamy Stock Photo; Chris Dorney/Alamy Stock Photo; Pierluigi Palazzi/Alamy Stock Photo; Courtesy of Claridge's **76–77** Hans L Bonnevier, Johner/Getty Images; WikiMedia Commons; Buyenlarge/Getty Images **78–79** Courtesy of the Hallmark Archives, Hallmark Cards, Inc., Kansas City, Missouri, USA; Bettmann/Getty Images; Hulton Archive/Getty Images; Time Life Pictures/Getty Images; Universal History Archive/Getty Images; Time Life Pictures/Getty Images; Smith Collection/Gado/Getty Images **80–81** Courtesy of the Hallmark Archives, Hallmark Cards, Inc., Kansas City, Missouri, USA (23) **82–83** Courtesy of the Hallmark Archives, Hallmark Cards, Inc., Kansas City, Missouri, USA (43) **84–85** IllustratedHistory/Alamy Stock Photo; knape/Getty Images **86–87** eli_asenova/Getty Images; Hybrid Images/Getty Images; Julie Vader/Shutterstock; Quanthem/Getty Images; Fritz, Albert/Getty Images; Iva Vagnerova/Getty Images; StockFood/Getty Images; DarcyMaulsby/Getty Images; Maria Popa Photo/Shutterstock; herain kanthatham/Shutterstock; grafvision/Shutterstock; ltummy/Getty Images; Stephen Gibson/Shutterstock **88–89** AFP/Getty Images; Zhanna Mendel/Shutterstock (2) **90–91** Newspix/Getty Images; MAURO PIMENTEL/Getty Images; INTERFOTO/Alamy Stock Photo; nito/Shutterstock **92–93** dpa picture alliance/Alamy Stock Photo; WikiMedia Commons; bilwissedition Ltd. & Co. KG/Alamy Stock Photo **94–95** Richard Wareham Fotografie/Alamy Stock Photo; Artur Lebedev/Getty Images; ART Collection/Alamy Stock Photo **96–97** NurPhoto/Getty Images; KAZUHIRO NOGI/Getty Images; DustyPixel/Getty Images; Alamy Stock Photo **98–99** Shutterstock **100–101** 20th Century-Fox Film Corporation/Everett Collection **102–103** Buena Vista/Everett Collection (2); Warner Brothers/Everett Collection **104–105** Warner Bros./Everett Collection (2); 20th Century Fox Film Corp/Everett Collection (2) **106–107** Michael Gibson/Netflix/Everett Collection (2); TriStar Pictures/Everett Collection; New Line/Everett Collection **108–109** Everett Collection; Buena Vista Pictures/Everett Collection; Allstar Picture Library/Alamy Stock Photo (2) **110–111** Dimension Films/Everett Collection (2); Pictorial Press Ltd./Alamy Stock Photo; Everett Collection **112–113** INTERFOTO/Alamy Stock Photo; WikiMedia Commons; The Picture Art Collection/Alamy Stock Photo; Art Collection 4/Alamy Stock Photo; Courtesy of Brandywine River Museum **114–115** Curtis Publishing/Saturday Evening Post; Courtesy of the Hallmark Archives, Hallmark Cards, Inc., Kansas City, Missouri, USA; Jeff Morgan 03/Alamy Stock Photo; Courtesy of Ed Wheeler **116–117** Courtesy of CBS; NBC/Getty Images; Everett Collection; Everett Collection (4) **118–119** Everett Collection (2); NBC/Getty Images **120–121** Everett Collection (3) **122–123** Everett Collection (4) **124–125** Warner Bros/Getty Images; Everett Collection; Hanna–Barbera/Everett Collection; NBC/Getty Images; Everett Collection; Courtesy of ABC; Warner Bros/Everett Collection; Courtesy of Fox Entertainment; Courtesy of NBC; AF archive/Alamy Stock Photo; Collection Christophel/Alamy Stock Photo; Everett Collection; Gale Adler/Fox/Courtesy/Everett Collection; MCA Television/Everett Collection **126–127** urbanbuzz/Alamy Stock Photo; Library of Congress/Getty Images **128–129** Anthony Pleva/Alamy Stock Photo; Chronicle/Alamy Stock Photo; Courtesy of Russell Stover; WikiMedia Commons; WikiMedia Commons; The Advertising Archives/Alamy Stock Photo **130–131** Transcendental Graphics/Getty Images; Courtesy of Duke University; Advertising Archive/Everett Collection; WikiMedia Commons; Heritage Images/Getty Images (2); Buyenlarge/

Getty Images **132–133** Popperfoto/Getty Images; Neil Baylis/Alamy Stock Photo; Courtesy of Mars Corp; Everett Collection; Neil Baylis/Alamy Stock Photo; John Frost Newspapers/Alamy Stock Photo; Courtesy of Kraft Foods **134–135** avid_creative/Getty Images **136–137** Brian Rasic/Getty Images; Harry Scott/Getty Images; Pictorial Press Ltd./Alamy Stock Photo; Pictorial Press Ltd./Alamy Stock Photo **138–139** Blank Archives/Getty Images; Michael Ochs Archives/Getty Images (2); PRNEWSWIRE.com **140–141** Getty Images **142–143** Bettmann/Getty Images; Getty Images; Bettmann/Getty Images; Everett Collection; Pictorial Press Ltd./Alamy Stock Photo **144–145** Vadim Georgiev/Shutterstock **146–147** Tetra Images/Getty Images **148–149** moodboard/Getty Images; Anneka/Shutterstock; photogal/Shutterstock; Marc Tielemans/Alamy Stock Photo; Pictures Now/Alamy Stock Photo; Marc Tielemans/Alamy Stock Photo **150–151** Bill Truran/Alamy Stock Photo **152–153** Andrew Paterson/Alamy Stock Photo; Getty Images; Shelly Still Photographer/Shutterstock; Yvonne Hemsey/Getty Images **154–155** Billion Photos/Shutterstock; Chris Willson/Alamy Stock Photo (4) **156–157** Chris Willson/Alamy Stock Photo (3); Nicescene/Shutterstock; AlexLMX/Shutterstock; Nicescene/Shutterstock; Carolyn Jenkins/Alamy Stock Photo; Chris Willson/Alamy Stock Photo (2); Ivan_Sabo/Shutterstock; Chris Willson/Alamy Stock Photo **158–159** David Crump/Daily Mail/Shutterstock; andrea crisante/Shutterstock; Chris Willson/Alamy Stock Photo; Nils Jorgensen/Shutterstock **160–161** Courtesy of Zillow (5) **162–163** Courtesy of Zillow **164–165** CSA Images/Getty Images; Visage/Getty Images **166–167** CSA Images/Getty Images; Stockbyte/Visage/Getty Images **168–169** deliormanli/Getty Images; athertoncustoms/Getty Images; Alexandra Grablewski/Getty Images; subjug/Getty Images; Jamie Grill/Getty Images; Lucie Lang/Shutterstock **170–171** Allstar Picture Library/Alamy Stock Photo; CSA Images/Getty Images; Everett Collection; ryasick/Getty Images; Oleksandr Rybitskiy/Getty Images; Greg Hensel/Alamy Stock Photo **172–173** Getty Images; Jupiterimages/Getty Images; Hulton Archive/Getty Images; PA Images/Alamy Stock Photo; smartboy10/Getty Images **174–175** CSA Images/Getty Images; DNY59/Getty Images; Lebazele/Getty Images; Jeff Johnson/EyeEm; uergen Sack/Getty Images **176–177** Yui Mok — PA Images/Getty Images **178–179** Yui Mok — PA Images/Getty Images; HollenderX2 **180–181** Al Bello/Getty Images; WikiMedia Commons; Al Bello/Getty Images; Peter Macdiarmid/Getty Images **182–183** Courtesy of Heather Shayne (2) **184–185** Courtesy of CJ THOMPSON (9); Courtesy of Heather Shayne **BACK FLAP** E+/Ramberg/Getty Images **BACK COVER** AndreyTTL/E+/Getty Images; Collection Christophel/Alamy Stock Photo; VIAVAL/Alamy Stock Photo; Everett Collection (3); Bettmann/Getty Images; Everett Collection; Greg Hensel/Alamy Stock Photo; Jamie Grill/Getty Images

SPECIAL THANKS TO CONTRIBUTING WRITERS

LISA CHAMBERS, KELLY FARRELL, ALICE KING, ANNE MARIE O'CONNOR, KATHLEEN PERRICONE

CENTENNIAL BOOKS

An Imprint of
Centennial Media, LLC
40 Worth St., 10th Floor
New York, NY 10013, U.S.A.

CENTENNIAL BOOKS is a trademark of Centennial Media, LLC

ISBN 978-1-951274-42-9
Distributed by
Simon & Schuster, Inc.
1230 Avenue of the Americas
New York, NY 10020, U.S.A.

For information about custom editions, special sales, and premium and corporate purchases,
please contact Centennial Media at contact@centennialmedia.com.

Manufactured in Turkey

1 0 9 8 7 6 5 4 3 2

Publishers & Co-Founders Ben Harris, Sebastian Raatz
Editorial Director Annabel Vered
Creative Director Jessica Power
Deputy Editors Ron Kelly, Alyssa Shaffer
Design Director Ben Margherita
Art Directors Andrea Lukeman,
Natali Suasnavas, Joseph Ulatowski
Assistant Art Director Jaclyn Loney
Photo Editor Jennifer Veiga
Production Manager Paul Rodina
Production Assistant Alyssa Swiderski
Editorial Assistant Tiana Schippa
Sales & Marketing Jeremy Nurnberg